THE EIGHTH VESSEL

Achieving Abundance and Balance by Following the Laws of the Universe

JENNA ZWAGIL

THE EIGHTH VESSEL

LEGAL DISCLAIMER:

This book is a work of historical fiction. Names, characters, places, and incidents either are products of the author's imagination or are used fictitiously. Any resemblance to actual events, locations, or persons, living or dead, is entirely coincidental.

The author has taken creative liberties in crafting this story and its characters. While some aspects of the narrative may draw inspiration from real-life experiences, historical events, or existing places, many have been altered, adapted, and reimagined to suit the fictional context of this work.

Readers are encouraged to approach this book with an open mind. The intent is to entertain, provoke thought, and stimulate imagination through the power of storytelling.

Thank you for choosing to embark on this fictional journey with us. We hope you find enjoyment and inspiration within its pages.

JENNA ZWAGIL

Published by

Success in 100 Pages

SuccessIn100Pages.com

ISBN 978-1-947814-59-2

Copyright © 2024

All rights reserved.

Except as permitted under the United States Copyright Act of 1976, no part of this publication may be reproduced, distributed, transmitted in any form or by any means, or stored in a data retrieval system, including photocopying, recording, or other electronic or mechanical methods, without the prior written permission of the author.

"The lips of wisdom are closed,
except to the ears of understanding."

— *The Kybalion*

TABLE OF CONTENTS

	DEDICATION...	6
	INTRODUCTION...	7
	PROLOGUE...	14
CHAPTER I:	Breaking Barriers...	16
CHAPTER II:	The Invitation...	21
CHAPTER III:	The Obsidian Mirror...	23
CHAPTER IV:	The Ancient Marketplace...	29
CHAPTER V:	Cast the Sorceress Out!...	34
CHAPTER VI:	Striking a Deal...	38
CHAPTER VII:	3,500 Years of History...	41
CHAPTER VIII:	The First Vessel (The Law of Mentalism)...	47
CHAPTER IX:	The Second Vessel (The Law of Correspondence)...	55
CHAPTER X:	The Third Vessel (The Law of Vibration)...	63
CHAPTER XI:	The Fourth Vessel (The Law of Polarity)...	71
CHAPTER XII:	The Fifth Vessel (The Law of Rhythm)...	79
CHAPTER XIII:	The Sixth Vessel (The Law of Cause and Effect)...	89
CHAPTER XIV:	The Seventh Vessel (The Law of Gender)...	97
CHAPTER XV:	Back to the Present...	105
CHAPTER XVI:	Returning to Egypt...	108
CHAPTER XVII:	The Speech...	112
	NOTES OF INTEREST...	114
	ABOUT THE AUTHOR...	117
	CONNECT WITH JENNA...	118

DEDICATION

To the Memory of
Bob Proctor

A good friend, an amazing mentor, and someone who was far ahead of his time.

INTRODUCTION

This book is designed to achieve one primary objective: To introduce you to the laws of the universe; laws that have become a centerpiece of my life. And the lives of many others.

It's important to point out that these laws do not compete with any religion, personal beliefs, or things you may have been taught in your church—*they are universal.* As the word implies, they apply to everyone, everywhere, all the time.

And while it should go without saying, adopting the concepts in this book will *not* make you part of a cult or otherwise "new age" beliefs. By definition, cults are relatively small groups of people devoted to a particular individual, set of beliefs, and often both. The people who lead cults are often delusionally evil. For example, the Doomsday cult. Heaven's Gate. The Manson Family. Jonestown.

Unlike cults, which people create, The Laws of the Universe have no creator or self-appointed leader. They didn't need one. Cults have a beginning and an end. The Laws of the Universe simply *are* and *always will be.*

Where These Laws Come From

The Universal Laws in this book are based on the Hermetic Philosophies contained in *The Kybalion*. So, as much as I'd love to take credit for them, I can't. There is nothing new here. *I didn't invent them.* They have existed forever, long before humans walked the Earth. They were written about thousands of years ago, in Ancient Egypt, ancient Greece, and many other cultures. Even when the knowledge of these laws disappeared from society, as they did for multiple centuries, they resurfaced again and again. They are universal laws, so it doesn't matter if you agree with them or not. Like gravity, they don't require your belief to work.

What I'm saying is that you can ignore these laws all you want, but eventually, there will come a time where, either consciously or unconsciously, you will have to be in harmony with them to sustain a peaceful, growth-driven life. Even if you don't believe in them, they operate regardless. These laws apply to you and every other form of energy—from a single atom to the tallest skyscraper, even the highest mountain.

The reason the Laws of the Universe matter is because they identify and describe the way things operate in the time-space reality in which we live. Think of them as the rules of the game. Or, if you prefer, think of them as the operator's manual for your life—the one you were never given.

Until now.

These laws do not compete with the Bible, the Quran, the Torah, or any other holy book, but rather help explain some of the phenomena in them.

These laws are *always* active, whether you are aware of them or not. Not recognizing them, understanding them, or using them, puts you at a significant disadvantage to those who understand, such as those who (think they) run the world, the elites, the higher-ups, and those in power.

The Seven Universal Laws

The Seven Universal Laws you will learn about in this book are:

1. The Law of Mentalism: The All is Mind. The Universe is Mental. Our reality is a product of our thoughts.

2. The Law of Correspondence: As above, so below. Everything is created twice, first in the mind and then in the physical.

3. The Law of Vibration: Nothing in the universe is truly at rest. Everything is made of energy, and all energy is in motion.

4. The Law of Polarity: Opposites are simply two extremes of the same thing. Understanding this duality is key to transcending it.

5. The Law of Rhythm: There are cycles and patterns in everything, from the rise and fall of civilizations to the rhythms of our daily lives.

6. The Law of Cause and Effect: Every cause has an effect, and every effect has a cause. Nothing happens by chance, and there is a reason for every event.

7. The Law of Gender: There is gender in everything, not just in terms of male and female, but also in terms of masculine and feminine qualities within all things.

These laws not only apply to us here on Earth. The entire universe follows the same laws. And they never change. They affect everyone, everywhere, all the time.

Hold a pen at arm's length, then let it go. Assuming you haven't glued the pen to your hand, I'll wager a million dollars it will fall down, never up. Every planet, moon, star, and black hole in the universe has gravity—more on some, less on others, depending on their size—but the laws of gravity exist everywhere.

Most of us take all of this for granted, that the universe operates according to predictable laws. The speed of light travels at 186,000 miles per second, no matter where it comes from or in which direction the light is headed. The light from a flashlight, or from the sun—or a star in a distant galaxy on the other side of the universe—all travel at the same speed. It's a mathematical certainty.

> *"The natural laws of the universe are so precise that we don't have any difficulty building spaceships, we can send people to the moon, and you can time the landing with the precision of a fraction of a second."*
>
> - Dr. Wernher von Braun

There are no mistakes in the universe. Miracles, which are unexplained causes, yes. But mistakes? No.

The Laws of the Universe are Absolute

Dependable, absolute laws govern the universe. And this is good. We need to understand that there is order in the universe to operate. Imagine going to bed at night not knowing what the rules will be in the morning. Hot things become hotter. Things fall up. You flip the switch on the wall, and it takes fifteen minutes for the room to fill with light. Then the next day, everything is different again. Living like this would be complete chaos.

Not only do we rely on the belief that the laws of the universe exist, we rely on the idea that they don't change.

So, why is the universe orderly? There are plenty of theologians, philosophers, and scientists who still wrestle with answering this question. For the sake of this book, you can draw your own conclusion. For our purposes here, all that matters is that it is orderly.

Can you survive without learning them? Sure. But why would anyone want to survive when they have the option to thrive?

Being Mentored by One of the Giants

I had the great fortune to be mentored by one of the greatest thought leaders of our time. His name was Bob Proctor.

Bob was a highly sought-after professional speaker, success coach, and *New York Times* best-selling author. If you asked him what his title was, he would tell you he was simply a teacher. He was best known, however, as a major contributor to the film, *The Secret*. As such, his teachings played a central part in the worldwide infatuation of The Law of Attraction. But it didn't start there.

In many ways, Bob was ahead of his time, committed to the idea that *positive thinking* can shape one's reality and that a *positive self-image* is the foundation for a positive life. Many people fought him early on in his career, saying that his ideas were *pseudoscientific, too mystical,* and *too simplistic* to work. That was then. Few people argue with Bob's understanding of these laws today.

Among the many things Bob taught me:

- Thoughts become things. If you see it in your mind, you can hold it in your hand.
- Faith and fear both demand you believe in something you cannot see. Fear is nothing but the absence of faith and faith based on understanding can move mountains.
- The only limits in our life are those we impose on ourselves.

- See yourself living in abundance and you will attract it. It always works, it works every time with every person.
- If you're unhappy with what you're getting, focus on what you're giving. Expressing gratitude now brings more good in the future.
- Our results are based on our paradigms or habits. Our results show us how we've been programmed. To change our results, we must change the programming within.
- Each of us can design our own lives.

Not only was Bob a good friend and mentor, he was also nice enough to write the foreword to my first book, *Breaking All the Rules*. So, to say that Bob had an impact on me is an understatement. In many ways, his teachings and his friendship changed my life.

Sadly, Bob left the earthly plane on February 3, 2022. I will forever be grateful that our paths crossed as they did and for the relationship we had. I can still hear Bob's voice in my head saying, "Energy cannot be created or destroyed, it simply moves from one form to another." Because of that, I know he is still very much with us among the stars.

Why I Wrote This Book as a "Fable"

When deciding to write this book, I knew the content it needed to have, but I didn't want it to sound like another textbook of the *Hermetic Principles*. There were enough books written that way already, and the thought of having these laws told through storytelling seemed like the perfect way to bring ancient wisdom into modern-day life and make it memorable for the reader.

There are a number of books on the Laws of the Universe already, and I saw no reason to write one that was simply a repeat of the others. While many of the books have good content, most of them are too long and, in many cases, slow and hard to read.

Fables captivate the imagination and convey important lessons in an engaging and memorable manner that endure through the ages and evoke emotions that can amplify the impact of the lessons contained within the story.

It is my intent for readers worldwide to wake up from the idea that life is happening to them and realize they are creating it as they go along and can change it at any time. And while *The Eighth Vessel* is a fictional story, the lessons contained within its pages are anything but.

PROLOGUE

The year was 1908, and a sign on the shop door said "Closed," but the man knew the door would be unlocked. His friend was a tireless worker and maintained long hours. He would be there. He reached for the door handle and pulled. It was open, as expected.

Above him, a bell dinged, and, before he was barely inside, the owner of the shop appeared. "William! How wonderful to see you. How are you feeling? Did you see the pyramids?"

"I did, but that doesn't matter," the man said.

"What do you mean it doesn't matter?" the printer asked.

The man pulled a manuscript out of a burlap bag and placed it on the table. "I need a favor."

"What is that?" the printer asked.

"It's something I accidentally brought back with me from my trip."

"Accidentally?"

"It's a long story. Suffice it to say, I was in a shop in Giza, haggling over the price of a cheap amulet, when I saw a large ceramic vessel, a vase, in colors of blue and gold. It was stunning. I couldn't take my eyes off it. For reasons I still don't quite understand, I purchased it for an ungodly sum. I didn't even try to haggle—I simply had to have it."

"Okay."

"When I got home, the cat ran underfoot, and I lost my balance. I dropped the vessel, and it shattered to the floor. When I looked down, I discovered a collection of scrolls written in Arabic hidden inside. I had the text translated, and—well, it's quite extraordinary."

"You want me to read it?"

"I want everyone to read it. I want you to publish it!"

"I'm not a publisher, I'm just a printer. I do advertising flyers and wedding invitations."

"You own a printing press, correct?"

"Well, yes. But..."

"But nothing. I'm hiring you to print something for me on that press of yours. It's no more complicated than that."

The printer thought for a bit, then said, "How many copies do you want?"

"As many as this can fetch," the man said, pulling an amethyst stone from his pocket and holding it out in the palm of his hand.

"And these books, what do I do with them?" the printer asked.

"Give them away. Give them to bookstores and libraries. Pass them out on the street to anyone and everyone who is willing to read it."

"You mean, for free?"

"Yes. This must be shared with everyone."

CHAPTER I:
Breaking Barriers

The set of CNBC's new show, *Breaking Barriers: Women in Business,* was buzzing with energy. No expense had been spared on the sleek, futuristic studio, showcasing the show name and CNBC logo in the background. What's more, to show its commitment to the show's success, the network had persuaded David Clayton—one of the most respected and polished news anchors in the business—to jump ship from a competitor and become the show's host.

Back in the green room, the featured guest, entrepreneur Lindsey Moore, responded to an important email from her assistant on her phone. Then she heard a voice from the doorway and looked up to see a young man standing there. "We're ready for you, Ms. Moore," the young man said.

Lindsey stood and checked her image in the mirror and adjusted her blazer. Her phone buzzed, most likely with another email. Whatever it was, it would have to wait. She was about to go on camera.

Lindsey was led to the stage where she was greeted by the host. "First time on television?" David asked.

"I've done a few shows," Lindsey responded, not bothering to mention that she'd appeared on TV over one hundred times, including having been a guest on his own show on his previous network just a year earlier.

"Well, don't let the pressure affect you," David said. "It's just you, me, and a few million viewers."

Lindsey looked around the studio and noticed that not only was the host of the show a man, but every other employee she could see was male. The irony that all the employees working on a women's business show were male was not lost on her. Change took time, she thought, but sometimes time moved way too slowly.

* * *

"So, Lindsey, you've achieved remarkable success at such a young age," David remarked once the cameras were on. "Can you share with our viewers the journey that brought you to where you are today?"

"Certainly, David. It all started with a passion for technology and a desire to make a difference. Like Steve Jobs and Steve Wozniak, I founded my company in a garage eight years ago. Unlike the Steves, I am not a techie. I had an idea but didn't know how to turn it into reality. So, I did what I had to do—I mortgaged my house and recruited a small team of brilliant engineers who I believed were innovation-driven and committed to solving a real-world problem."

"Impressive," David said. "And the problem your company solves is what…?"

"Real-time, instantaneous language translation," Lindsey said.

"Doesn't that exist already?" David asked. "I mean, I can talk into my phone and Google translates what I say."

"True enough," Lindsey agreed. "But our device has a built-in power source that doesn't need to be recharged for seven days and is small enough to fit in your ear. Try doing that with a cellphone."

"Sounds like a fancy hearing aid," David chuckled.

"It's not a hearing aid, David, it's a communication aid."

"Okay, what's it called?"

"It's called LanguaSync," Lindsey said.

"I don't suppose you brought this LanguaSync device with you to demonstrate it for us, did you?"

"I'd be a pretty bad entrepreneur if I didn't," Lindsey said, pulling a small black device from her pocket, holding it out toward the camera, then placing it in her ear.

"That's it?"

"Yep, that's it."

"Not exactly Elon Musk level stuff, is it?"

"You mean because Elon is planning on colonizing Mars?"

"Exactly."

"When he does, who do you think will be going? People from every country on Earth. And how do you think all these people are going to communicate with each other, David?"

"Are you telling me…?"

"Yes. My company already has contracts with SpaceX and NASA. LanguaSync is being used by the astronauts on the International Space Station as we speak." Lindsey produced a second device and instructed David to place it in his ear. "Do you speak a foreign language?"

"I took French in high school, does that count?" David asked.

"It does if you remember any of it. Say something in French, anything."

"Okay. Voudrais-tu aller à la bibliothèque avec moi ce soir?"

Lindsey immediately responded: "No, David, I do not want to go to the library with you tonight."

"Wow, that's amazing!" David said.

"Do you speak Greek?" Lindsey asked.

"Not a word," David said.

"Good. Giatí den échete gynaíkes stin omáda paragogís sas?"

David listened to the translation in his ear, then turned beet red. "We'll be back after a few short commercial messages from our sponsors."

Lindsey had just asked David why he didn't have any females working on his production crew, and it was clear he got the message.

* * *

After the show returned from the commercial break, David Clayton—who was clearly annoyed by Lindsey's question—went on the attack.

"This is the part of the show where we shift from business and let our viewers learn about the personal side of our guests. So, Lindsey, when you're not busy changing the world, how do you spend your time? Any hobbies or interests?"

The question caught Lindsey off-guard. She'd been so busy, she hadn't done her homework and taken the time to watch the show before coming on. It wasn't like her to not be prepared.

"Well, there's not much to tell."

"Really? I read somewhere that you spend a good deal of your free time dabbling in the occult," David said. "Is that true?"

"*The occult?*"

"Yes, you know, things like the spiritual laws of the universe and other 'new age' stuff," David pressed.

"I don't know where you get your information, David, but the Laws of the Universe are *scientific* in nature. There's nothing new age about them."

"So, you do believe in the power of manifestation and all that *everything-in-the-universe-vibrates* stuff," David said flatly.

This was not a place Lindsey really wanted to go, especially on a business show, but she was trapped. She did believe in the power of universal laws that had clearly been used to guide her journey. "'The Seven Spiritual Laws of the Universe' have served as my guiding principles," Lindsey said. "They're about more than just business; they're about living in harmony with the world around us. Understanding them helps us recognize our infinite potential as humans and gives us basic instructions for how to get what we want out of life. I encourage everyone to explore these laws with an open heart and mind."

CHAPTER II:

The Invitation

Lindsey was sitting at her desk, reviewing a contract offer from a foreign government to license her LanguaSync technology, when the phone rang. It was a number she didn't recognize, but she decided to answer it anyway. "This is Lindsey Moore, who is this?" she asked.

"Yes, Ms. Moore, I'm so glad I was able to reach you," a woman said. "My name is Nien-Wei, and I saw your interview on the *Breaking Barriers* show on CNBC. It was very impressive."

"If you're calling about licensing, let me give you the number for our business development department."

"Actually, I'm reaching out for a different purpose," the woman said. "I'm calling to see if you'd be interested in speaking at our upcoming conference in Las Vegas."

"I'm flattered, but I really don't do speaking engagements to promote LanguaSync."

"Oh, no, this has nothing to do with your company's product," Nien-Wei said. "We're inviting you to speak about how you used the 'Spiritual Laws of the Universe' to achieve success in your life."

Lindsey was still a bit embarrassed about how David Clayton had trapped her into talking about her spiritual beliefs, so the invitation was unexpected and appreciated. "Tell me about your conference," she said.

"The conference is for aspiring female entrepreneurs, and this year's theme just so happens to be 'Timeless Wisdom for Future Success,' and you'd be perfect! Our group is fairly small, just 100 people, but everyone in the room is an *up-and-comer* in their respective industries. You'd be the keynote speaker. Please say yes."

"When is the conference?" Lindsey asked.

"Well, that's the thing," Nien-Wei said. "It's only a month away. The keynote speaker we originally hired had to cancel, so we're in a bit of a bind."

"A month from now?" Lindsey said. "That doesn't give me much time to prepare."

"Prepare? What's to prepare?" Nien-Wei said. "Just come and tell your story. I don't know why, but I think there's a reason you're supposed to be our speaker—so many stars had to align for this. First, our speaker canceled on us. Second, I just happened to see your cable interview. And third, the conference is at the Luxor, right here in Vegas. The whole thing feels like divine intervention, wouldn't you say?"

"You're quite a salesperson," Lindsey said. "I'll be there."

JENNA ZWAGIL

CHAPTER III:
The Obsidian Mirror

Despite being told there was no need to prepare for the speech she'd just agreed to give, Lindsey was still feeling a bit foolish for not having done her homework prior to her guest appearance on the *Breaking Barriers* show. Determined not to let it happen again, she decided to work on the speech. When she was done, she headed home.

Nestled in Summerlin, a suburb of Las Vegas, Lindsey's 12,000-square-foot house sat on a private golf course, surrounded by the desert's natural beauty and with a view of the lights of the Vegas strip.

Lindsey pulled her Dodger Blue Lamborghini Urus into the garage and noticed her husband's car wasn't there. She looked at her watch and saw it was 9:20 p.m. Then she glanced at her phone to see if there were any text messages. There weren't.

Jack was a high-powered lawyer on the verge of becoming a partner at Bennett, Turner & Walsh Law Group in Las Vegas, and while he worked long hours on a regular basis, it was unlike him not to leave her a message that he was going to be late.

Lindsey pressed a button on her cell phone and waited. The call went straight to voice mail. "Hey, it's me, I'm home. Where are you? Call me, huh?"

Two minutes later the phone rang.

"Hey, Linds, I'm sorry for not calling. I'm stuck with a client who wanted to have dinner at Bobby Flay's new steakhouse," Jack said.

"You're still at dinner? Now?"

"No," Jack said. "After we finished eating, the client insisted that I join him for a cigar. We're at the Montecristo Cigar Bar, but we should be wrapping up soon."

"Who's the client?" Lindsey asked.

"Maxwell Barrington."

Barrington was the firm's biggest client, and saying no to the man was not an option. "Well, don't get into a car with him if he's drinking."

"Don't worry, I won't," Jack said. "I'll be home as soon as I can."

Jack clicked off, and Lindsey wished she could have told him about the event she'd just been asked to speak at. She'd have to tell him in the morning.

* * *

After having a quick bite to eat, Lindsey went to her walk-in closet to select an outfit that would make a statement for the upcoming speech. There was no need to choose the outfit so far in advance, but she was a fanatic for prepping ahead of time.

After considering several options, she chose a tailored, double-breasted Gucci blazer in a rich, deep navy blue. To go underneath, she found a silk Chanel blouse in a soft ivory color. She'd bought the blouse because she loved the delicate ruffles on the neckline and cuffs but had never had the chance to wear it. Now, what to do for slacks?

Lindsey decided years earlier to opt for pants over skirts or dresses. She felt pants were more comfortable and provided greater freedom of movement. And long gone were the days when women *had* to wear dresses to be deemed professional.

One of Lindsey's other quirks was that she hated carrying a purse. It was simply another thing to keep track of. The pants had pockets, which made it easy to carry her keys, wallet, and phone. She'd yet to find a skirt with functional pockets large enough for her needs.

Lindsey found the other things she'd need; a sleek pair of black-leather, red-soled Christian Louboutin stilettos, a chunky gold Cartier necklace, to add a touch of glamour and draw attention to her neckline, and a red and navy Givenchy scarf. Finally, she grabbed a pair of Tiffany stud earrings, a sleek gold Bulgari bracelet, and a tube of bold red lipstick, sliding them all into the pocket of her blazer.

It had been a while since Lindsey had worn the items, so she decided to try on everything to make sure they fit perfectly. If not, she'd have time to get it tailored. Lindsey put on the outfit and stood in the mirror. She felt the look exuded a sense of sophistication, elegance, and taste. The jacket might need to be taken in a pinch at the waist, but otherwise, it was perfect.

Before she forgot, Lindsey went to her office and found four fully charged LanguaSync devices and slid them into her blazer pocket with the other accessories she'd chosen. If there were people who spoke different languages in the audience, she could demonstrate how multiple people can use the system all at once.

* * *

Lindsey thought about the speech notes she'd made earlier in the day and knew she only had about 30 minutes of content, but the speech was an hour. She needed to add something else to the presentation. What about the Akashic records, she wondered?

The "Akashic Records" is a concept that suggested there was a kind of *cosmic library* that contained ancient wisdom, including every thought, action, and event that has ever occurred in the past, present, or future. Thank God she hadn't mentioned this on the *Breaking Barriers* show—the host would have had a field day.

Were the Akashic Records real? Lindsey couldn't say. She believed they were real, but try as she might, she'd never been able to access them herself. She'd tried to use meditation, visualization, and hypnosis. She'd even tried something called scrying.

Scrying, a spiritual practice with roots in Ancient Egypt, involved gazing into a translucent bowl of water, a crystal ball, or a candle flame—anything that could put one in a trance and allow them to travel to other places and times. All without success.

Lindsey glanced at her watch. It was 10:40 p.m. If she was in bed by midnight, she'd get six hours of sleep before getting up for the day. Six hours was all she needed. She decided to use the time to try again.

* * *

Lindsey made her way up the stairs to the third level of the house, which consisted of three extra bedrooms, one of which Lindsey called the "meditation room."

The walls of the room were painted in calming, earthy tones; soft blues, muted greens, and warm beige, chosen to create a soothing backdrop for spiritual activities. The floor was made of polished bamboo, with a large plush rug in the center that provided a comfortable, warm surface for sitting or kneeling. The room was illuminated with soft lighting from Himalayan salt lamps and candles.

Overhead, the ceiling featured a set of skylights that lit the room with natural light by day but also allowed Lindsey to see the stars on clear nights, even with the light pollution from the Vegas strip.

The meditation room was sparsely furnished, with a single wooden chair and a small altar against one wall, adorned with spiritually significant objects: crystals, incense burners, and a statue of the Great Sphinx of Egypt, which Lindsey had visited with Jack on their fifth anniversary. She could only imagine what it was like in Ancient Egypt during those times.

But the most important feature, standing in the far corner of the room, was the obsidian mirror Lindsey used for scrying. Admittedly, she'd yet to achieve success and couldn't say she traveled anywhere. However, she did feel dizzy and disoriented on several occasions, a common experience for people who tried their luck with astral projection.

Amid the moonlight filtering through the skylight, casting eerie shadows on the walls, Lindsey stepped in front of the mirror, closed her eyes, and took a deep breath. Then, she began repeating:

> *"Through this mirror, I seek to find,*
> *the realm beyond all space and time.*
> *As above is so below,*
> *take me where I'd like to go."*

After repeating the incantation for the third time, Lindsey watched in awe as the mirror deepened even further as if it were becoming an even darker shade of black. Her heart began to race in her chest. Was it actually happening? She didn't know. All she knew was she'd never gotten this far before.

Suddenly, the black mirror began to radiate a soft, ethereal glow, and the room around her seemed to blur and waver. Lindsey felt herself being pulled forward toward the mirror by some invisible force as if she were being physically drawn into the glass. To steady herself, she instinctively leaned forward and placed her hand on the mirror. And then it happened.

CHAPTER IV:
The Ancient Marketplace

To steady herself, Lindsey had reached forward, placing her hand on the mirror, and a moment later she found herself lying on the ground, looking up at a clear blue sky and a scorching hot sun.

Lindsey bolted upright. She looked around, wide-eyed, and saw she was in the heart of what appeared to be some kind of ancient marketplace.

Lindsey pulled herself to her feet and peered through the dusty air, which was thick with the scent of spices and exotic perfumes. Colorful stalls constructed from reeds and palm fronds lined narrow streets and exotic goods filled every available space. She marveled at the sights and sounds, her senses overwhelmed by the vibrant scene in front of her. Shoppers in elaborate linen robes shouted at merchants in a language she didn't understand, haggling over loaves of bread, gemstones, exotic fruits, and intricately woven textiles. Lindsey instantly knew she had somehow been transported back in time.

The journey through the blackened mirror had taken her to a place she could never have imagined. She wanted to make the most of the extraordinary moment she found herself in. On the other hand, she was terrified. And she had a problem.

THE EIGHTH VESSEL

Lindsey's fair skin, blonde hair, plus the outfit she was wearing made it impossible for her to blend in. She needed a place to hide and gather herself until she could figure out what to do next.

Suddenly, a woman dressed in a flowing linen robe approached, her eyes filled with curiosity and suspicion. "Min 'anti? Limadha 'ant huna?" the woman said.

"I'm sorry, I—I don't speak your language," Lindsey said.

"Min 'anti? Limadha 'ant huna?" the woman said louder this time. Lindsey didn't know what the woman was saying, but she assumed it had something to do with her appearance. Lindsey did the only thing she could think of and slowly walked away from the woman.

Lindsey heard the woman continue to shout from behind and saw people turn in her direction and look at her. In a panic, she started running, pulling the scarf from around her neck and wrapping it around her head to hide her blonde hair. She spotted a merchant's stall piled high with robes. She hurried to the table, grabbed a plain ivory-colored robe, and pulled it over her head. She tried to sneak away, but the merchant saw her.

"Quf! Lis!" the merchant screamed. "Quf! Lis! Quf! Lis!"

Lindsey flashed a quick look of apology but kept walking. She'd have to find a way to pay her debt later.

The robe was heavy and hot, especially since it was over her other clothing, and Lindsey started sweating profusely. She glanced up at the scorching sun and knew she had to get inside somewhere. Then she saw the guards. And they saw her. She had no choice but to start running again.

Desperately weaving through the maze of stalls in a state of panic, with the guards closing in behind her, she spotted an alleyway and raced toward it. She turned the corner, placed herself with her back flat against a stone wall, and waited. Several seconds later she heard the guard's sandals slapping against the dusty ground as they approached. And then they ran past.

Lindsey tried to calm herself, but her heart was pounding and her breath came out in ragged gasps. Meditation was a whole lot easier when you weren't filled with fear.

Finally, her breathing under control, Lindsey reached down and removed her shoes. Running in them had been a nightmare, and even though the ground was hot—even in the shade—being barefoot had to be better than the stilettos if she needed to run again. She also removed the robe but decided to keep it, draping it over her arm in case she needed it again.

Now she had a decision to make: Go back to the marketplace, or continue down the alley? She decided to head down the alley.

* * *

Lindsey navigated her way through the labyrinth of narrow alleyways but felt more and more lost. Was she going in circles? Was she heading back to the market, or getting further away? She had no idea.

Eventually, Lindsey came upon some kind of temple covered with intricate carvings, reliefs, and what she immediately recognized as hieroglyphics. Was she in Egypt? Perhaps. But if that was the case, it clearly wasn't modern-day Egypt—it was Ancient Egypt! But how? How was it possible? There was only one answer. She'd traveled there through the mirror. What other explanation could there possibly be?

Like every other building she'd passed, the temple was built of what looked like either sandstone or limestone. Unlike the other buildings, the front of this one had a set of six large columns, three on either side, and two large marble obelisks that towered upward toward the sky.

Lindsey decided to take a chance and entered through the doors, finding herself in a large hall, filled with statues—the walls covered in more hieroglyphics. Large windows allowed beams of sunlight to fill the room. It was awe-inspiringly beautiful.

At the far end of the room, Lindsey found two sets of stairs. One stairway went up, the other down. Which way to go? Lindsey wondered. There was no way to know. It was a coin flip. She went down.

As she descended the stairs, the light faded behind her until she entered another room, lavishly decorated with more statues of Gods and Pharaohs, made from granite and precious metals. At the back of that room was yet another doorway, which led to a narrow hallway lit by rows of oil lamps set into fixtures in the walls.

Lindsey followed the hallway until she found a chamber, dimly lit by the flickering glow of a single oil lamp on a wooden table. Sitting at the table were a man and a woman, dressed in robes, busily writing on papyrus scrolls.

The man was wearing a long white tunic, made of what looked like linen or wool, with a purple cloth belt cinched at the waist. On his feet, he wore leather sandals, similar to those being worn by the guards that had chased her through the market.

The woman wore a long, flowing red gown that appeared shiny in the candlelight; it was probably silk, Lindsey thought. Like the man, the woman had a sash cinched tightly at the waist, creating a more fitted look that accentuated her figure. She was adorned with various types of jewelry, including necklaces, bracelets, rings, and earrings. She was obviously a woman of stature.

They were talking to each other, but Lindsey had no idea what they were saying. Then she remembered she'd put four of the LanguaSync devices in her pants pocket. Were they still there?

Lindsey lifted the robe she'd stolen and slid her hand into her pocket. Yes, they were there. But did they work? Each device had its own built-in microphone and power source and didn't require Wi-Fi. Even if they worked, did the engineers program this language, which she assumed was some form of Egyptian Arabic? There was only one way to find out.

Lindsey placed one of the devices in her ear, pressed the *on* button, and held her breath. She paused, concentrating on their voices, and to her amazement, it worked! The translations weren't perfect, but good enough that Lindsey got the gist of what they were talking about.

Lindsey stood in the darkness of the doorway to the sanctuary, watching in fascination as the two people toiled away at their tasks. The scene reminded her of the Spaceship Earth ride at EPCOT. On the ride there was a scene set in an ancient civilization, where scribes were sitting at tables, painstakingly recording information on scrolls.

In this case, the scribes were real, engaged in their work right before Lindsey's eyes. But, on the ride, the animatronic scribes didn't suddenly stop what they were doing, turn, and look at you.

CHAPTER V:

Cast the Sorceress Out!

The woman shot to her feet and grabbed a dagger that was lying on the table, then took a step toward the doorway and thrust it in Lindsey's direction. The woman shouted at Lindsey, and Lindsey heard the LanguaSync translation in her ear: "Who are you?" the woman asked. "By whose decree do you dare to appear in this sacred chamber?"

"I'm sorry," Lindsey said, raising her hands, instinctively apologizing, even though she knew they couldn't understand her.

The woman raised an eyebrow, her scrutiny intensifying. "She may be a foreigner, or perhaps something else?"

"Remain calm, Tiye," Lindsey heard the man say in her ear. "Put the dagger down."

Lindsey now knew the woman's name: Tiye.

"Her attire is unlike any I have ever seen," Tiye continued. "I believe she is a spy, Hermes, from a rival kingdom, or worse—look at her manner of dress! And she carries weapons!"

Weapons? What was she talking about? Lindsey wondered. She looked down to see she was still carrying the Christian Louboutin stilettos in her hand. "They're not weapons, they're shoes," Lindsey said. But she realized how the four-inch heels might be mistaken for something someone could stab someone with, and she tossed them to the ground.

Lindsey knew the only way she could communicate with them would be to give them LanguaSync devices. She stepped slowly forward, her hands still held in the air, then reached into her pocket. Tiye lifted the dagger again and pointed it at Lindsey, who slowly pulled two of the LanguaSync devices from her pocket and held them up for Tiye and Hermes to see.

"What—?" Tiye said in Hermes' direction.

"Wait," Hermes said.

Lindsey removed her scarf and turned her head, so Tiye and Hermes could see the device in her ear. Then she took several additional steps forward and laid two LanguaSyncs on the table. Lindsey pointed at the devices, and then at the device in her ear.

Hermes and Tiye looked at each other, but neither of them picked up the devices.

Lindsey removed the LanguaSync device from her own ear, held it up, and then placed it back in her ear. "Don't worry, it's safe. They won't hurt you."

* * *

Hermes lifted one of the devices from the table and placed it in his ear. Tiye did not follow his lead.

"Do you hear me?" Lindsey asked.

Hermes took a step backward in wonderment at what was happening. "Yes, I hear your words," Hermes said. "How is this possible?"

"This is used to communicate where I come from," Lindsey said.

Hermes lifted the other LanguaSync device from the table and held it out to Tiye. "Place this in your ear, Tiye," he said, pointing to his ear.

Tiye reluctantly took the device from Hermes and did as she was instructed. "It does nothing," Tiye said.

"Hello, Tiye, I'm pleased to meet you," Lindsey said, then watched a look of astonishment spread across Tiye's face.

"How do you know my name?" Tiye asked.

"I heard you both say your names," Lindsey said. "You are Tiye, and he is Hermes."

"She is a sorceress with unnatural powers!" Tiye shouted. "She does not belong, Hermes. She must be cast out!"

"I am not a sorceress," Lindsey said calmly. "But you are right, Tiye, I do not belong here. I come from a different place, in a different time," Lindsey said.

"A different time? A lie!" Tiye spat. "I tell you, Hermes, I am right—this one is a spy. She—"

Hermes held up his hand, cutting Tiye off. Then he turned to Lindsey and said, "You claim you are from a different place and a different time? Explain yourself."

Lindsey knew two things for sure: The first thing was, Hermes was the one in charge. The second thing was that it was too early to elaborate. "Not now. I will tell you everything you want to know later. Right now, I need your help."

"What is the nature of the help you seek?" Hermes asked.

"I have nowhere to go. I need a place to stay for a while. Will you let me stay here?"

"Never," Tiye scoffed. "You must leave."

"I can't leave," Lindsey said. "They are looking for me, the guards."

"Why do they seek you?" Hermes asked.

Lindsey held up the robe and said, "Because I took this from a seller in the marketplace—without paying."

"And a thief!" Tiye spat. "We should turn her over to the authorities and let them handle the matter."

Silence filled the room as Hermes considered the situation. "The guards report to the Pharaoh, and I am the Pharaoh's representative," he said. "In this case, I alone have the power to decide what becomes of her, not the guards. I want to know where she comes from, and the nature of these tools that allow us to speak to each other. Until then, we are best served by keeping her presence to ourselves. For now, she may stay."

Lindsey exhaled and started to cry. So much for being the strong woman who could handle any situation, she thought. "Thank you," Lindsey said. "In time I will tell you everything you want to know. I promise."

Hermes nodded and said, "What is your name?"

"My name is Lindsey."

"Lindsey," Hermes repeated. "If you've come from far away, you must be thirsty and tired." Hermes turned in Tiye's direction and said, "Tiye, show Lindsey to a room where she can shelter and get her some bread, figs, and honey."

"Perhaps I should get her a bowl and water so she can bathe herself clean? She looks like a dirty pig."

Hermes looked at Tiye, his anger flashing in his glare. "Lindsey is our guest, Tiye. You will treat her accordingly." Then, to Lindsey: "You may be our guest, but make no mistake, we will watch your every move."

CHAPTER VI:

Striking a Deal

Lindsey woke from what she assumed was a bad dream. But when she opened her eyes and looked around the sparse room, from her place on the reed-mat bed on the floor, she realized it was no dream. She had somehow managed to travel across space and time to Ancient Egypt. She had no idea what city she was in, or what year it was.

There was no one to blame, of course, because the situation was completely of her making. As the saying goes: *Be careful what you wish for because you just might get it.*

Lindsey found her personal belongings on a small table and was relieved to see everything was there. She picked up her cellphone and pressed the *on* button and was surprised to see it light up. Otherwise, it was useless. When she'd finished getting dressed, she placed one of the LanguaSync devices in her ear and smiled.

The invention had worked beyond anything she could have hoped for. Fortunately, of the 200 languages built into the device, Arabic was one of them. The translations were imperfect due to changes to the language over the millennia, but close enough to be understood.

Lindsey crossed the room and pulled on the door handle to discover it was locked. She was a prisoner, and she knew why.

Tiye.

Lindsey pounded on the door and yelled, "Hey, let me out of here! Let me out!" No response. No one came. She returned to her reed-mat bed and sat back down. There was nothing to do but wait.

* * *

Several hours passed before Lindsey heard the door being unlocked. It was Hermes. "I'm sorry to have locked you in, but Tiye insisted. I hope you slept well."

"Tiye thinks I'm a spy or some kind of sorceress," Lindsey said.

"Tiye is under great pressure."

"Pressure? Pressure over what?"

Hermes wouldn't fully say, other than it had something to do with the Pharaoh.

"Who is the Pharaoh?" Lindsey asked.

"You don't know?" Hermes said.

Lindsey shook her head, no.

"Thutmose III."

Lindsey knew a bit about Egyptian history but wasn't knowledgeable enough to place when Thutmose III lived. "Is Thutmose related to King Tut?"

"I have never heard of this King Tut," Hermes said.

Lindsey felt her heart begin to beat faster. She knew King Tut lived in 1,300 BC. If Hermes had never heard of him, the time they were in had to be earlier than that.

"There's something you're not telling me," Lindsey said.

"What would cause you to say that?" Hermes asked, raising an eyebrow.

"Call it women's intuition," Lindsey said. "It feels to me like Tiye is hiding something. What is it?"

Hermes remained silent, then said: "If you tell me the truth about who you are and how you came to be here, I will tell you what you wish to know. Are we agreed?"

Lindsey felt her stomach twist in uncertainty. Explaining that she was a time traveler from the future was risky, especially if Tiye found out. The woman already thought she was a sorceress. On the other hand, what other choice did she have?

Lindsey turned to face Hermes and, looking him directly in the eye, said, "Agreed."

CHAPTER VII:
3,500 Years of History

I know this will sound impossible, but I come from the future," Lindsey started.

"The future?" Hermes repeated, clearly skeptical.

Lindsey realized that saying she was from the year 2024 would be meaningless since her calendar was based on the birth of Christ, who had yet to be born. "I am from a time 3,500 years from now," she said finally, "in a country called America."

Hermes remained silent.

Lindsey pointed to the LanguaSync device in her ear and said, "Have you ever seen anything as magical as this before? No, you haven't. And why? Because nothing like this exists in your time, it hasn't been invented yet. We have advanced tools, which we call 'technologies,' that are beyond your wildest imagination."

Once again, Hermes remained silent, considering what he was being told. Then he said, "To my mind, there could be no other explanation."

"So, you believe me?" Lindsey said, surprised.

"What choice do I have?" Hermes asked. "Tell me, how did you get here to this place and time?"

"I used a technique, something called 'scrying.'"

Hermes' expression opened in recognition. "Mystics in our time use this process to gain insights into the past, present, or future. It is done by gazing into a pool of water or a candle flame."

"I used a blackened mirror, but it has the same effect," Lindsey said. "One moment I was looking in the mirror, and the next thing I knew, I was lying on the ground in the market. To be honest, I didn't expect to physically be able to time travel—if I did, would I have dressed like this?"

"That is mysterious! There must be a reason for it," Hermes said, then added: "Tell me about this future of yours."

Lindsey had a decision to make: What to share and what not to share?

Lindsey found her knowledge of history put to the test. She started with the time of Jesus and the spread of Christianity, the rise of Islam, the Byzantine Empire, and the Crusades in the 11th to 13th centuries. She skipped the Dark Ages and went to the Renaissance and the period of Enlightenment in the 18th century. She decided to leave out the atomic bomb, chemical weapons, and social media, because she found it too embarrassing to admit knowledge and technology in the future would be used in such disgusting and destructive ways.

Hermes listened with rapt attention and amazement, then asked: "What other miracles exist—what did you call them, technologies?"

"Yes, advances in technology change the world in many ways," Lindsey said. "In general, they've made life easier and more comfortable, at least for most people."

She described electricity, the telephone, the automobile, the radio, the TV, the computer, and the internet, all to the man's astonishment. But the thing that made Hermes gasp was when she told him about the invention of the airplane.

"Is this true?" Hermes asked. "Are you telling me man masters the skies?"

"Yes. Not only that, in 1969, we put a man on the moon," Lindsey said, "and—"

Lindsey was about to tell Hermes that a man named Elon Musk was working on colonizing Mars, but she stopped mid-sentence when she saw the tears streaming down Hermes' face."

"I'm sorry, I know it's a lot to take in," Lindsey said.

"It's fine," Hermes said. "No, it's beyond fine, it's wonderful. Thank you."

"It might be best if you keep this to yourself," Lindsey said.

"I understand. What you've shared stays with me."

* * *

Having felt she'd kept her end of the bargain, it was time for Hermes to keep his. "Are you ready to tell me what's going on? Everything I told you was true—now it's your turn."

"Yes, we have an agreement," Hermes started. "There is a hierarchical structure in Egyptian society. The divine ruler, the Pharaoh, is at the top. He holds absolute power. Beneath the Pharaoh, there are the nobles, followed by priests and scribes. After that, there are artisans, laborers, and slaves."

"What does this have to do with you?" Lindsey prodded.

"I am the Pharaoh's chief scribe, Lindsey, an important and esteemed position in our society. I am responsible for recording religious texts and preserving the knowledge of the Gods. It is my job to capture the thoughts, musings, and wisdom of the ages—secrets that include alchemy, astrology, magic, mysticism, and more—passed down through the millennia from Pharaoh to Pharaoh."

"That's what you and Tiye are working on?" Lindsey asked.

Hermes nodded.

"This is why Tiye is so anxious?"

"If I share it with you, you must vow to keep it to yourself. An accidental word could cause great turmoil for our people."

"I won't say a word to anyone," Lindsey said. It was an easy promise to make; after all, who could she possibly tell?

"The Pharaoh, King Thutmose III, is dying."

"Oh, I see."

"The transition from one Pharaoh to the next is a difficult time, filled with fear and uncertainty for our subjects. There is often fighting and bloodshed as the elites vie for superiority and power."

"How long does the Pharaoh have to live?"

"Days, perhaps a week, and the Pharaoh wants me to transcribe The Seven Laws of the Universe and have them ready for burial with his body in the Valley of the Kings."

* * *

Although Hermes had promised to keep her secret, Lindsey couldn't assume he would; after all, if *she* met someone from a different place and time, could she keep her lips sealed? If he *did* tell someone, it would most likely be Tiye.

"I understand Hermes told you the Pharaoh was dying," Tiye said when she arrived at the scriptorium. To Lindsey's relief, there was no mention of time travel. "That means he trusts you, and if he does, so shall I."

"I appreciate that," Lindsey said, feeling a sense of guilt for not trusting Tiye with the truth.

"What did Hermes tell you about himself?" Tiye asked.

"Nothing, really," Lindsey said, realizing she'd spent hours talking about the world in the future while having asked nothing about Hermes' past. "Tell me."

"Hermes Trismegistus is a great man, yet a humble man—too humble, at times," Tiye said. "He tells others he is merely a scribe, responsible for recording the wisdom of the Pharaoh. Truth be told, it is Hermes who has the wisdom. The Pharaoh is nothing but a figurehead, with little in his head. Being part of a bloodline of elites does not make one intelligent—rich and powerful, perhaps, but wise? I think not. Without Hermes by his side, Pharaoh Thutmose III would be insignificant."

"I imagine this is not the type of thing one says to the Pharaoh's face," Lindsey said. "If you did—"

"If one did, they'd be dead, and so would Hermes, himself," Tiye said. "Hermes goes along with the Pharaoh's wishes because he feels he has no choice."

"It seems like the smart thing to do," Lindsey said.

"Smart, yes. But courageous? Do not twist my words into something they are not—I am Hermes' most loyal disciple, a true believer in his greatness—but I fear it is he who will go down in history as the footnote, while that fool Thutmose receives the glory."

"If Hermes would be killed, as you say, what exactly would you have him do?" Lindsey asked.

Tiye did not respond. Either she had no answer, or she did but preferred not to share it.

"I'm not sure what he should do," Tiye said. "The Pharaoh's laws dictate knowledge be reserved for the elites, but I see the suffering of the common people every day. The people thirst for wisdom, for guidance, but they are held back. The knowledge being withheld could bring enlightenment to all. Knowledge should be shared, not hidden away in the shadows."

"What are you suggesting?" Lindsey said.

"I am suggesting nothing," Tiye said. "I am merely voicing my anger at what is, at the expense of what could be."

Chapter VIII:
The First Vessel

The Law of Mentalism
"All Is Mind; The Universe Is Mental."

To Lindsey's surprise, Tiye had arranged for her to be moved to a room that was twice the size, with a mattress made from straw, covered with linen fabric. As she lay there, staring at the ceiling, she contemplated her situation.

Lindsey had been in Egypt for less than forty-eight hours, but so much had transpired that it felt like forty-eight days. And she had only just discovered where in Egypt she was—in the city of Thebes, on the banks of the Nile River. If she remembered correctly, Thebes was later renamed Luxor.

Lindsey was embarrassed at how little thought she'd given to what her husband, Jack, must be going through. She pictured him coming home and finding her gone. No note. No text or voice mail message. No nothing. And this was after she'd chastised him for not calling to let her know he was going to be home late from work. She could only imagine his concern and panic. How was she going to get home? She needed a plan.

Just then there was a knock on her door, and she found Hermes standing there. "Good morning," he said. "I thought you'd like to see the first of the seven vessels. It has just arrived."

"The seven vessels?"

"Come, I will explain."

Lindsey followed Hermes to the scriptorium where they'd first met and found Tiye waiting for them, holding an ornately decorated vase adorned with intricate designs and symbols.

"It's beautiful," Lindsey said. "And there are seven of these?"

"There will be by the end of the week," Hermes said. "This is the first to be completed."

"Tell her about their purpose," Tiye said.

"The seven vessels represent the Seven Laws of the Universe," Hermes said. "The Pharaoh wishes to have each of the laws written on parchment scrolls, with each of the scrolls placed in separate vessels."

"Why?" Lindsey asked.

"The vessels are to be buried in the Pharaoh's tomb in the Valley of the Kings when he passes," Tiye said, the disdain for the Pharaoh etched on her face. "By doing so, he can take the knowledge with him into the next life."

"He is the Pharaoh, Tiye. It is his prerogative."

"He is a selfish buffoon," Tiye said.

"Watch your tongue," Hermes said.

"Why? Because you will turn me in for my insolence?" Tiye spat.

"Not me. But if your hatred for the man were to fall on the wrong set of ears, even I may not be in the position to save you."

* * *

"Why do you call this a vessel rather than a vase?" Lindsey asked once Tiye had left the room.

Hermes replied, "Both vases and vessels are containers, the difference is in their intended purpose. Vases are for holding flowers or plants for short periods of time. Vessels store substances of great importance for longer durations."

"Like a body is a vessel for the soul?"

"Precisely," Hermes said. "A vessel can be a container for emotions, love, and spiritual beliefs."

"Or in the case of the laws of the universe, they can be vessels for knowledge," Lindsey said.

"True."

"This first vessel, what great wisdom is it intended to hold?"

"The first vessel is for the first law of the universe, which is 'The Law of Mentalism: All Is Mind.' Everything one perceives—everything that exists—is merely a creation of the mind. The universe is a mental construct, a product of divine thought and intention. Even what we call reality is the product of thought," Hermes said.

"Reality is the product of thought?" Lindsey said. "I'm not sure that's true."

"What is your definition of reality?" Hermes asked.

"Reality is what's real, as opposed to what is purely imaginary," Lindsey said.

"Ah, imagination, such an interesting topic," Hermes said. "What is your definition of imagination?"

"I'd say imagination is seeing things that are not actually present in the real world."

"Very well. Would you say this room is real?" Hermes asked, waving his arm.

Lindsey looked around, then said: "Of course."

"How do you know?" Hermes said. "How do you know you're not just imagining it?"

It was a good point. When she first arrived, Lindsey considered the idea that her situation wasn't real; that she was in a computer-generated construct, like in the movie, *The Matrix*.

In the movie, the main character, Neo, comes to realize he's living in a holographic, pseudo-reality. Neo starts seeing behind the code—the facade. He realizes everybody around him is programmed to simply go along. Nobody's thinking for themselves. They're living in a computer-coded rat race. Once Neo starts to see beyond the fakeness of the matrix, he comes into his own empowerment.

"At best, the reality you describe is a subjective one, based on your own perceptions," Hermes said. "I am asking you about the objective reality of the world. You see the world through one lens, I see it through another. Which one is real?"

"Both," Lindsey said.

"The answer is neither," Hermes replied. "There is no such thing as 'objective reality.' All reality is subjective, as perceived through the eyes of the individual."

* * *

Lindsey thought about The Law of Mentalism and how the idea that "All is Mind" was playing out in the modern world with virtual and augmented reality. The more we interact with digitally simulated environments, the more blurred the line between physical and mental reality. So why would it be any different in the universe as a whole?

"Perception is reality?" Lindsey said.

"Yes. Every perception we have of the world is shaped by one's mental filters—one's beliefs," Hermes said. "The way we interpret what we see, hear, smell, touch, and taste. Without our senses, we cannot perceive the world. Reality is totally subjective. It varies from person to person. Everything in the universe, including the physical world and all observable phenomena, originates from the realm of the mind, or what we call consciousness. Most people think the physical world is reality, and the spiritual world is fiction, when in fact, it is the other way around. The spiritual realm is the primary reality, and the physical world is merely a manifestation or reflection of our mental processes, energized by our spirit within."

Lindsey had always believed that people could use their minds to create their reality. Hermes was saying everything in existence is but an image in the Universal Mind. This reminded Lindsey of a passage she read in the Bible, Genesis 1:27: *So God created man in his own image, in the image of God He created him; male and female he created them*—the word image coming from the word imagine—suggesting God created man mentally from his own Universal Mind.

"The Law of Mentalism reminds us that the underlying substance of the universe is consciousness itself," Hermes said. "Let me ask you: When you die, does the world still exist?"

"Of course, it does," Lindsey said.

"Really? How will you know?"

"Well, I guess I won't, but—"

"When you die, *your* world ceases to exist because the world was in your mind," Hermes said. "When I die, *my* world will cease to exist for the same reason. The question is: What if everyone were to die? Would there be a world at all if there were no minds to perceive it? Since energy cannot be created or destroyed and can only be transmuted, some believe when you die, you're free of this world but can now be released into another existence, dimension, lifetime, or experience."

This reminded Lindsey of the age-old question: *If a tree falls in the forest and there is no one there to hear it, does it make any sound?* From a scientific standpoint, the falling tree generates vibrations that travel through the air, but an ear—a receiver—is required for sound.

"So, you're saying that without the Universal Mind, the world doesn't exist at all?" Lindsey said.

"Yes. That is correct," Hermes said. "All we perceive, experience, and interact with is a product of our mind. Everything, from the tiniest particle of dust to the brightest star in the sky, is shaped by the creative power of the mind. Cogito, ergo sum."

"I think, therefore I am," Lindsey said.

"You've heard it before?"

"Yes, it's a quote from René Descartes, in the 1600s."

Hermes smiled but said nothing. Then it hit her: How could Hermes have known the saying in *1400 BC* if it hadn't been coined until 3,000 years later? The answer was obvious: Descartes had gotten the quote from Hermes, not the other way around.

* * *

"People take the mind for granted," Hermes continued. "They treat the mind as if it were air or water. We take air and water for granted because they are readily available. They are free, and anything given for free is undervalued. What's more, because the human mind is given to us for free at birth, we think nothing of it. If we had to build or buy a mind, it would be different."

Hermes had a point. From her experience, people never value that which comes easy.

"Making the conscious decision to harness the power of our mind allows us to maximize the creative potential of our thoughts, beliefs, and intentions," Hermes continued. "And in doing so, we become active participants in shaping our reality as opposed to being reactive victims of the universe."

"Few people consciously choose their thoughts," Lindsey said. "When you get your thoughts and emotions in alignment with your long-term goals and desires, you can manifest—*or bring about*— miracles in your life."

"I agree," Hermes said. "Everything is fiction, until it becomes real, and everything we perceive as real is also fiction. Everything that exists in this world is created twice, first in the mind, and then in reality. This vessel is an example. Someone had to *think* it into existence."

"Let me stop you there," Lindsey said. "I'm on board with the idea that thoughts become things, but those thoughts have to be coupled with action. You can't just *think* your way to results, you must also *do*."

"Very perceptive," Hermes said with a smile. "But thought always comes first before anything is manifested in physical form."

"But thoughts are not real things," Lindsey said.

"Are you sure?" Hermes asked, raising an eyebrow.

"Well, if we can weigh our words, can we not also weigh our thoughts?"

JENNA ZWAGIL

Chapter IX:
The Second Vessel

The Law of Correspondence
"As Above, So Below; As Below, So Above."

Lindsey woke in the middle of the night, tossed and turned for a while, then got up and dressed. She found Hermes at work in the dimly lit scriptorium, a flowing robe draped gracefully around his shoulders, his movements deliberate and methodical as he scratched words on parchment paper with a feathered quill dipped in ink. The candles used to light the room during the day had been replaced by an oil lamp.

"Sit, I am almost finished," Hermes said without looking up. Several minutes later he stood and said, "Let us take a walk."

Lindsey's stomach growled and she hoped the walk Hermes had in mind would take them somewhere they could get food. To her surprise, he took her through a door that led outside the temple, and they stepped into the darkness. She gazed upward toward the sky, unblemished by the glow of artificial lights that revealed the true brilliance of the stars as they once were. The Milky Way stretched from horizon to horizon like a million diamonds in a way Lindsey had only seen in photographs. "My, God, I've never seen the sky like this."

"Are there no stars to be seen in the sky in the future world?"

"Yes, we have stars, but the lights from our cities make them hard to see," Lindsey said. "Oh, there's Orion's belt."

"You know the constellations?"

"I used to know them all," Lindsey said.

"Our ancestors have navigated the deserts and the river for thousands of years by these very stars. I am pleased to know they are still in the sky in your time, even if their beauty is obscured."

"I'm guessing you have a reason for bringing me out here," Lindsey said.

"I thought we could talk about the second law of the universe," Hermes said. "It introduces the correspondence between the different planes of existence."

"Planes of existence?"

"Close your eyes and think of a memory from your childhood. Do you have one?"

"I have it," Lindsey said.

"As you recalled the memory, where were you? Your body was here, but your mind was elsewhere, on another plane."

Lindsey thought about some of the classes she had in high school, how boring they were, and how she couldn't wait to get out of there. She spent most of her time daydreaming. She was there physically, but not mentally.

"There are three planes of existence. The first is the Physical Plane where our bodies and the tangible world exist. It includes everything we can perceive with our senses. The second is the Mental Plane, which is the realm of thoughts, ideas, emotions, and intellectual activities. This plane is where our consciousness resides. The third and final plane is the Spiritual Plane, associated with our higher selves."

"Our souls?" Lindsey asked.

* * *

"Yes," Hermes said. "The Spiritual Plane transcends the physical and mental planes and connects us to a broader universal consciousness or divine source. It is where spiritual growth, enlightenment, and higher wisdom are explored. The Law of Correspondence says these planes are interconnected, and that changes or influences in one plane can affect the others. Even the smallest act in one has an impact on the others."

Lindsey told Hermes about a movie called *The Butterfly Effect* in which a seemingly small event, like the flap of a butterfly's wings in London, could set off a tornado in Kansas.

"Your movie is correct," Hermes said. "The world is like a spider's web; touch it anywhere, and you set the whole thing trembling."

"My husband, Jack, suffers from debilitating back pain every time he has a stressful case at the law firm he works at," Lindsey said. "And before I go on stage, I am literally sick to my stomach from nerves. My mental anxiety brings about a physical response."

"A perfect example of the correspondence between the planes," Hermes said. "The mind often creates physical pain or disease as a signal from our emotions. All things operate on these three planes."

"Like?"

"Water. It can be a liquid, but it can also be ice or steam. Three different planes of the same thing."

"What about trees?" Lindsey said. "They don't exist on a mental plane, because trees can't think."

"True, trees can't think," Hermes said, "but we can think of trees. In that way, they exist in the mental plane. Trees were once mere seeds that were programmed by a thinking universe or Mind of God to become a tree."

"Do you think the universe thinks?" Lindsey asked. "Are you saying there is logic to the universe?"

"Of course. And do you know what that logic is?"

Lindsey assumed Hermes was going to say, "God," but instead, he told her: "Mathematics is the language of the universe, and it speaks to us in every way imaginable—in every pattern, shape, and structure. The deeper you look, the more math you will find. There are mathematical constants everywhere—in art, nature, and architecture, from the vast cosmos to the tiniest piece of dust and even from the spiral patterns of a nautilus shell to the proportions of the human body. Mathematics is the signature of God."

"The human body is based on math?" Lindsey asked.

"Yes, I'll show you."

* * *

Hermes led Lindsey back to the scriptorium and lit several candles, then said, "Wait here."

Hermes returned with a tall mirror which he leaned against the wall. The mirror was unlike anything Lindsey had ever seen, made from copper that was hammered into a thin, flat sheet and polished to create a reflective surface.

"Stand before the mirror and tell me what you see," Hermes instructed.

Lindsey stepped forward and gazed into the unforgiving surface of the mirror. Her eyes, once bright and full of life, were now sunken and hollow, with dark circles heavy beneath them. Her skin was drained of its vitality by days of little food, limited sleep, and relentless stress. Her hair hung limply around her face, devoid of its usual luster. And her lips, usually painted with shades of confidence and allure, were now chapped and pale. "I see that I should have packed some moisturizer before teleporting to the desert," she said, trying to mask the embarrassment of her appearance with humor.

"Look deeper, Lindsey, beyond the superficial," Hermes said. "Study your features and tell me what you see."

Lindsey studied the features of her face and thought she understood. "I see balance, I see symmetry," she said.

"Yes, each side of the face mirrors the other, but there's more," Hermes said. "Every aspect of our features are based on a mathematical premise called 'The Golden Ratio.' The distance between the top of your head and the chin, where your eyes are positioned—the distance between the pupils of your eyes, the width of your nose and mouth, your hairline, and eyebrows—not a single thing is placed where it is by accident. Everything follows a predictable mathematical formula. Come to the desk, I'll show you."

Hermes grabbed a blank sheet of parchment, dipped his quill into the inkwell, and began to draw until he'd created what looked like a series of geometric shapes.

"What does this mean?"

"It's an illustration of a simple math sequence, created by adding each number to the previous result: 0+1=1, 1+1=2, 2+1=3, 3+2=5, 5+3=8, 8+5=13, 13+8=21, and so on."

"Okay, what does it mean?"

"Here's what it looks like," Hermes said, drawing on the parchment. "What does that remind you of?"

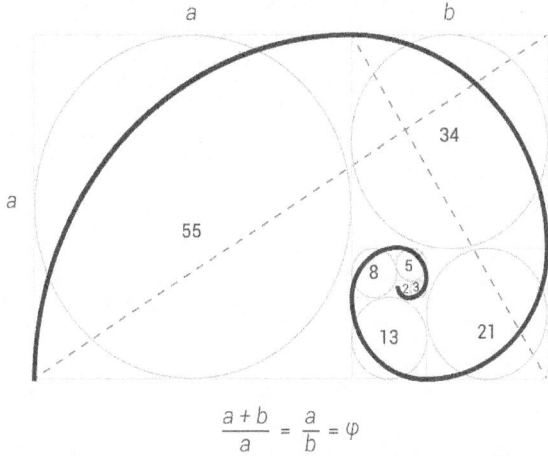

Lindsey wanted to say it reminded her of flunking geometry in high school, but then she saw it: "It looks like one of those seashells, what do they call them, nautilus shells?"

"Yes," Hermes said. "This sequence of numbers is found everywhere in nature. It's in the spirals found in pinecones and sunflowers, in the seed patterns of fruits and vegetables, in the number of petals on flowers, in the branches and leaves of trees, and in the rings of growth on the tusks of elephants. It is present in every aspect of your body—the arms, the legs, right down to your feet. Make a fist and look at it from the side. What do you see?"

"It looks like the drawing of your formula," Lindsey said. She realized it also looked like the patterns of hurricanes, cyclones, and spiral galaxies—things Hermes would have no understanding of in the year 1400 BC and something she'd have a hard time explaining. But he was right: *As above, so below; as below, so above.* "The Law of Mentalism, which we talked about yesterday, seems connected to The Law of Correspondence."

Hermes smiled and nodded. "Perceptive. If you believe that you are small, if you believe that you are weak, if you believe you are poor, if you believe you are sick, those thoughts and beliefs will correspond in the physical world. If you believe these things to be true, you will act as if they are true..."

"...and then they will eventually become true," Lindsey said, finishing the thought.

"Nothing in this world is positive or negative—*they simply are*. It is the *person* who paints a thing with a positive or negative brush by assigning meaning to it. To the person with a positive mind, even the most tragic events in life can find the positive," Hermes said.

"And to the person with a negative mind, even the most beautiful things in life can be seen as negative," Lindsey added.

"Everything one sees in the world corresponds to the beauty or ugliness they carry inside of them. Like the stars in the sky tonight..."

"They were breathtaking!" Lindsey interjected. "Their beauty almost made me cry."

"That is because you carry beauty inside you," Hermes said. "The stars are neither beautiful nor ugly, they are simply stars. For one to change the way they see the stars, they must change what's inside of them."

JENNA ZWAGIL

Chapter X:
The Third Vessel

The Law of Vibration
"Everything Is in Motion; Nothing Is at Rest."

THE EIGHTH VESSEL

Lindsey was standing in the corner of her living room at home, watching as a pair of FBI agents interrogated her husband, Jack. *Where is your wife, Mr. Moore? Did you have a fight? Was it an accident?* "I'm right here!" Lindsey called out. "He didn't do anything to me. I'm right here!" They ignored her. *What did you do with her body?* the FBI Agent pressed. *Tell us the truth and things will go better for you.* Suddenly, a bell started ringing. One of the FBI Agents pulled his gun from his holster and pointed it at Jack...

Lindsey opened her eyes and pulled herself from the dream as the sound of a bell shook the temple from somewhere overhead. She quickly got dressed and made her way to the scriptorium where she found Tiye seated at the table. "What is that bell?" Lindsey asked as the sound reverberated through the chamber.

"Today is the start of the Feast of the Wadi," Lindsey heard Tiye say through her LanguaSync device. "The festival is an important religious and cultural event, honoring our deceased ancestors by making offerings to Anubis, who controls matters related to death, mummification, and the afterlife."

"Offerings?" Lindsey asked, hoping the word wasn't a euphemism for *sacrifice*.

"Gifts," Tiye said. "Bread, beer, wine, incense, fragrant oils, lotus flowers, clay figurines, and, if the person is of ample wealth, jewelry and amulets."

The ringing of the bell subsided, and Lindsey could hear music coming from above them. "Can I see it? Will you take me?"

Tiye led Lindsey up three flights of stairs to an area of the temple she had yet to see. They emerged on a balcony that overlooked the temple's main hall.

Lindsey watched in amazement as hundreds of celebrants danced in the flickering light that came from rows of torches hanging from the walls. A priest and priestess appeared, dressed in flowing white linen robes adorned with symbols. It was like watching something out of a Hollywood movie.

* * *

Once Lindsey and Tiye had retreated to the quiet of the scriptorium, Tiye said: "Hermes asked me to share the third law, The Law of Vibration, with you. What do you know about it?"

"I understand the general idea," Lindsey said, not wanting to overplay her knowledge. She was a big fan of the movie, *The Secret*, which was built around The Law of Vibration.

"The Law of Vibration states that everything vibrates, and nothing is at rest," Tiye began. "The manifestations of matter, energy, mind, and even spirit, come from varying rates of vibration. Those who understand the principle of vibration hold the scepter of power in their hands."

Lindsey was shocked that such an understanding existed so long ago. Most people would assume knowledge about atoms, and quantum mechanics were discoveries of modern science, not Ancient Egypt. How did they know so much?

"When you touch a solid object, like a table or a chair, it feels solid and stable. It is not. Rocks, trees, plants, and humans, all are made of particles of energy in constant motion. They are all made up of the same stuff—the only difference is their vibrational states. Motion is manifest in everything in the universe. The illusion that things are stationary and solid may be difficult for the mind to grasp, but I assure you it is so. Everything moves, nothing rests."

The conversation shifted to the topic of vibrational frequencies, and how like attracts like. "My husband and I talk about this all the time," Lindsey said. "We believe we are good together because we're on the same frequency. Our vibrations match."

"It is a proven fact," Tiye said. "The vibrational frequency of your thoughts attracts the people and circumstances that resonate with that frequency into your life. People with consistently positive thoughts and emotions are far more likely to attract positive experiences into their lives, and, conversely, negative thoughts almost certainly attract negative people and experiences."

Lindsey thought about how when she bought her car, the Lamborghini was pre-loaded with SiriusXM satellite radio, which had over 300 channels that were available instantly, simply with the push of a button. Each station was operating at a different frequency. All she had to do was choose the one she wanted. The irony that the system was called SiriusXM—with Sirius being a star the Ancient Egyptians used to guide them to the destination they wanted—was not lost on her.

* * *

"May I share a tale with you?" Tiye asked, handing Lindsey a small bowl of figs.

"Yes, of course," Lindsey replied, devouring the fruit.

"There was once a girl named Amina, born into a growing family in a small village on the banks of the Nile. Life in the village was harsh, and food was scarce. Amina's father, Ahmed, was a kind-hearted man who loved his family deeply. He worked tirelessly as a farmer, but despite his efforts, he struggled to provide enough food. As Ahmed watched his children grow weaker and thinner, he made a difficult decision."

Lindsey held her breath, fearing what Tiye was about to say.

"Ahmed sat down with his wife and told her the agonizing decision he had made: To sell their eldest daughter, Amina, into slavery in the city of Thebes. Amina's mother understood the gravity of their situation. They had six other children to care for, and they were desperate. With heavy hearts, they agreed it was the only thing they could do."

"That's horrible," Lindsey said.

"The following day, Ahmed and Amina embarked on the long journey to Thebes. As they approached the city, Amina was filled with fear and sadness. She had heard stories of the bustling metropolis and the grand temples dedicated to the gods, but she never imagined she would come there as a slave."

* * *

"What happened then?" Lindsey asked, engrossed with the story Tiye was telling her.

"Once they arrived in Thebes," Tiye continued, "Amina was sold to a man named Sennedjem. Amina slept in a room with twenty-two other slaves, male and female, in the worst conditions. But each night, after toiling away in the unforgiving Egyptian sun, Amina would lay on her back on a thin reed mat and dream of a better life as a free person. She imagined herself dressed in fine garments, wearing jewelry, and eating from golden trays filled with luscious fruits and bread. While others around accepted their situation, Amina held the vision of her freedom in her mind's eye.

"Time passed, and Amina's dedication and intelligence caught the eye of Sennedjem. Recognizing her potential, he decided to teach her to read and write, a privilege not afforded to most slaves. Amina soaked up knowledge like a sponge, and her wisdom and intelligence became known throughout the city.

"One day, as she was assisting Sennedjem with a particularly important trade negotiation, Amina caught the eye of a nobleman named Amunhotep. Impressed by her poise and intelligence, Amunhotep offered to buy her from Sennedjem at a generous price, and after much negotiation, the deal was struck. Under the care of Amunhotep, Amina's life changed dramatically. She was no longer a slave but rather a trusted advisor to a nobleman. Her influence and wisdom extended beyond the walls of his estate and reached the highest echelons of Thebes. Though she now slept in a straw-stuffed bed covered in fine linen sheets and ate the foods of royalty, there was still one more dream that had gone unfulfilled."

"What was the dream?" Lindsey asked.

"Amina dreamed of becoming a scribe, where she could spend her days learning the ways of the elite, mastering the laws of the universe, and sharing that wisdom with the common people, so they could lift themselves from their circumstances."

"When did you change your name to Tiye?" Lindsey asked with a slight smile.

"I didn't know that what I was doing was an actual process—I simply thought of it as wishful dreaming," Tiye said. "Hermes told me what I did—creating a vision of what I wanted and holding it in my mind's eye and refusing to let that vision go—has a name. It's called visioneering."

* * *

Tiye spent the next hour showing Lindsey how to create mental images of desired outcomes, with an emphasis on coupling those images with emotions. "Emotions are the key to visioneering," Tiye said. "People believe that merely wishing for something will make it so. In our culture, we bake round cakes to symbolize the moon, place candles on it, and then blow them out in the belief that the smoke from the candles will carry our prayers to the gods."

"We do the same thing for birthdays," Lindsey said.

"Do these wishes come true? No. Why don't the wishes come true? The first reason is that such wishes are made quickly and then quickly forgotten. The second reason is such wishes are not coupled with emotion. Emotions increase the intensity and clarity of the wished-for desire. When I laid in the room as a slave, staring at the ceiling, my wishes were driven by strong emotional desire. Without the emotions I felt at the time, my wishes would be as meaningless as tossing a coin into a well and then thoughtlessly going about my day."

Lindsey considered Tiye's observation to be a valid one and had to admit that she had made many wishes that did not come true, for the exact reason Tiye pointed out.

"People from our time believe in the use of amulets and talismans that have protective and wish-fulfilling properties," Tiye said as she slipped her hand into the pocket of her robe. "The scarab beetle is an amulet that represents protection, transformation, and good luck."

Tiye placed a carved scarab in Lindsey's hand. "It's beautiful," Lindsey said. "What is it made of?"

"It's ivory," Tiye said. "It was hand-carved and given to me by the man who bought my freedom. I wish you to have it."

"Oh, no, I can't accept this, it's—"

"I insist," Tiye said. "When you first arrived, I believed you to be a spy or sorceress. I even threatened you with a dagger. I now know how wrong I was. Please take it."

As Lindsey took the scarab from Tiye, a wave of embarrassment washed over her, fueled by the realization that she had so severely misjudged the woman. As much as she believed women could do anything a man could do, she'd allowed her own preconceived notions to cloud her judgment. She'd unfairly assumed Tiye was little more than an assistant who couldn't possibly possess the knowledge of Hermes. How wrong she had been. At that moment, Lindsey vowed to do better.

JENNA ZWAGIL

Chapter XI:
The Fourth Vessel

The Law of Polarity
("Everything Is Dual; Everything Has Poles.")

THE EIGHTH VESSEL

"Eat, then join us," Hermes said, handing Lindsey a plate of fruit and biscuits. "And wear the sandals you were given—the banks of the Nile are rocky and uneven."

"The Nile?" Lindsey said, but Hermes ignored her and walked off.

Lindsey ate, got dressed, and found Hermes and Tiye in the scriptorium. "Why are we going to the Nile?"

"Have you ever made a vessel?" Tiye asked.

"Pottery?" Lindsey asked, confused. "No."

"Don't worry," Hermes said. "Tiye will teach you."

"But first we need to fetch more clay," Tiye said, handing Lindsey a red head scarf. "You'll need to hide your hair."

Tiye retrieved two burlap sacks filled with digging tools from an outside shed and led Lindsey in the direction of the marketplace. It was still early morning, but the air was already thick with humidity. Lindsey didn't care, she was just happy to be outside.

Walking through the marketplace was uneventful, at least compared to when she first arrived. Wearing a robe and with the scarf covering her blonde hair, she looked like any other citizen.

By the time Lindsey and Tiye arrived at the river, the sun was high up in a clear blue sky and already unbearably hot. The river was bustling with activity, with women kneeling on woven mats, scrubbing their garments, and rinsing them in the cool, clear water, as fishermen in boats cast their nets nearby.

Tiye led Lindsey to a steep area of the riverbank, away from the water's edge. "This is a good place," Tiye said.

The clay was buried beneath a top layer of wet, muddy soil. It was also sticky, hard, and surprisingly heavy, which made gathering it a labor-intensive process. Fortunately, Tiye had brought handpicks made from animal bone and showed Lindsey how to break up the compacted clay to loosen it from the ground.

"Soil is black," Tiye said. "Dig until you see the color turn to reddish-brown." After a few hours of collecting the clay, Tiye showed Lindsey how to remove sticks, stones, and other impurities. Once the sacks were full, Tiye suggested they start their way back to the temple.

"Can we rest a bit first?" Lindsey asked. She was physically exhausted, and her shoulders ached. She could only imagine the suffering Tiye must have endured as a slave.

* * *

The idea that she was sitting on the banks of the Nile River—centuries before the birth of Christ—was so surreal. "How far is it across the river, to the other side?"

"A thousand cubits," came the answer via the LanguaSync device. Lindsey recognized the flaw in the programming. It should have automatically translated the measurement of cubits to feet, yards, or miles. It was something she would fix, assuming she was ever able to return.

"How long is a cubit?" Lindsey asked.

Tiye pointed first to her elbow, then to the tip of her middle finger. "From here to here," Tiye said.

Lindsey guessed the length to be somewhere between 15 to 20 inches. How dependent modern-day humans had become on exact units of measurement, and electronic devices like calculators and cell phones and laptop computers, she thought.

"What do you think the people on the other side of the river call this side of the river?" Tiye asked.

Lindsey thought about the question for a moment and had to laugh. "Well, I guess they call *this* the other side of the river."

Tiye smiled and said, "The Law of Polarity teaches us that everything can be looked at from different perspectives. All things have 'two sides,' 'two aspects,' 'two poles,' a 'pair of opposites.' The river provides enlightenment on how there are always two sides and two perspectives of any single thing."

Lindsey thought of something her mother used to say, something she'd considered to be nothing more than a silly little poem. Now she could see her mother had been sharing a great truth.

> *"In a world of wonder, so vast and wide,*
> *There's a secret that we mustn't hide.*
> *There's a truth, my dear, we can't ignore,*
> *There are always two sides, and maybe more."*

"All opposites arise from the same source and are part of the unified fabric of existence," Tiye continued. "Recognizing the underlying unity of all things allows us to transcend the illusion of separation and cultivate oneness and interconnectedness. We think we are different from others, but the distance between us is merely an illusion of separation."

"Illusions of separation," Lindsey repeated. It was a phrase that perfectly described the division between people in the modern world: left and right; progressives and conservatives; black and white; rich and poor—all suffering from the illusion of separation. It was easy to demonize others who looked at the same thing as us but from a different perspective.

"The world is a dance of opposites," Tiye said. "Hot, cold; wealth, poverty; health, illness; war, peace; day, night; joy, sorrow."

"Up, down; inside, outside; empty, full; life, death; success and failure," Lindsey said, surprised at how quickly the pairs of opposites presented themselves.

"Imagine trying to live life without the existence of opposites," Tiye said. "I challenge you to state an example where the world would function more effectively without an opposite."

* * *

"What about good and evil?" Lindsey asked when Tiye challenged her to come up with an example of a pair of opposites where the world would be better without one of the two. "Certainly, you think the world would be better without evil, right?"

"I suggest you reconsider your position," Tiye said.

"You think the world is better because there is evil in it?"

"Ra, in his infinite wisdom, created both good and evil—not because he wanted to, but because he *had* to. We praise God for creating the light, yet we ignore the fact that God also created the darkness. Without the darkness, how could the stars possibly shine?"

It was a tough pill to swallow, but Lindsey knew Tiye was right. The universe is in cosmic balance, like yin and yang. It could be no other way. Without the bad times, good times would have no meaning. The Law of Polarity recognizes both. The key is to harvest the good in all. The hard times teach us great lessons and build us into who we need to become in order to achieve great harmony.

"Let me share a fable Egyptians tell," Tiye said. "Once there was an elderly farmer who had one son and one horse to plow the fields, grow their wheat, and transport the crop to market. Without the horse, they'd have no way to make a living.

"One day the horse broke through the fence and ran away. When neighbors heard this, they said: 'This is such bad fortune. Why have the Gods cursed you so?' The farmer shrugged and said, 'Curse or blessing, it is too soon to tell.'

"Days later the horse returned, but the horse wasn't alone. He had brought two wild horses with him. When the neighbors heard, they declared: 'You now have three horses, how blessed you are!' Again, the farmer said, 'Curse or blessing? It is too soon to tell.'

"Because the new horses were wild, they needed to be broken, and the task went to the son, who—while trying to mount one of the wild horses—fell and broke his leg. Now the neighbors declared: 'How terrible! The Gods have cursed you!' And once again, the farmer said: 'Curse? Blessing? Who knows?'

"A few days later, the Pharaoh's men rode into the village. A war had started, and they were enlisting the eldest son from each family to join the army and fight the enemy. When they came to the farmer's house, they did not take the son due to his broken leg, for he was of no use to them."

"Let me guess," Lindsey said. "Everyone said how blessed he was."

Tiye smiled and said: "The Law of Polarity teaches that whatever we experience can be looked at from different perspectives. No matter the situation, no matter how bad it may appear, there is always a silver lining to be found. The ability to find it can change your entire life."

Lindsey thought about how the Chinese used a single symbol for *crisis* and *opportunity*. How many fortunes were made by a few brave people during recessions, while the rest of the world whined about how bad times were? In that way, bad times were often the drivers that stimulated innovation and creativity. The truth is, everything just is. Nothing is good or bad, it just is. We assign our own meaning to things. We make things good or bad by our own association.

Tiye continued: "Those who can train themselves to postpone judgment and look for the good in all can transcend the limitations of life and free themselves. Unlike the immutable laws of the universe, The Law of Polarity is mutable."

"Mutable? What do you mean?"

* * *

Mutable laws can be influenced by human action, they can be transcended," Tiye explained. "The first three laws of the universe, however—the laws of mentalism, correspondence, and vibration—are immutable. They are absolute and unchanging. They are laws of nature that cannot be altered by any known means."

"Like gravity."

"I don't know what that word means, so I cannot say," Tiye stated.

"Gravity is the force that makes water flow downhill and causes things to fall when you drop them," Lindsey said. "It's the size and weight of the Earth and the pull it has on things."

Lindsey wondered if she had just stepped on the slippery slope of having shared too much information. "Explain how you could know the size of the Earth," Tiye said.

Yep, Pandora's Box was officially open. Lindsey had told Hermes that she was a traveler from the future; was she about to tell Tiye?

A day earlier, Tiye had shared the intimate details about her origins as a slave. Did she owe it to Tiye to tell the truth about where she was from? It was a big decision. Doing so could be dangerous.

In the end, Lindsey told her everything.

JENNA ZWAGIL

Chapter XII:
The Fifth Vessel

The Law of Rhythm
"Everything Flows Out and In;
Everything Has Its Tides."

When Lindsey arrived at the scriptorium the following morning, the air was thick with tension, and she immediately sensed something was wrong. "What's up, did someone die?" Lindsey said half-jokingly. Hermes and Tiye exchanged glances, but neither spoke a word.

Finally, Tiye cleared her throat and said: "The Pharaoh's health has taken a turn for the worse. He is gravely ill and has summoned Hermes to the Valley of the Kings."

"I'm sorry," Lindsey said softly.

"I'm not," Tiye said. "Egypt will be a better place with him gone."

"That's enough, Tiye," Hermes said.

"I speak the truth, Hermes, and you know it."

"I said, enough!" Hermes snapped.

Tiye's face turned a crimson color, and she stormed from the room, leaving Lindsey alone with Hermes.

"How far away is this place, the Valley of the Kings?" Lindsey asked. "When will you be leaving?"

"Not far, less than a day's travel on the other side of the river."

"I want to go!" Lindsey said.

"This would not be wise," Hermes said.

"You said it's not very far," Lindsey said. "Plus, I've traveled outside the temple several times without raising suspicion. Please take me with you."

Hermes released a deep breath. "We'll leave within the hour. Don't make me regret this decision."

* * *

Hermes and Lindsey approached a small boat dock on the edge of the Nile, the morning sun reflecting in a mesmerizing dance of light and shadows on the water. There in the sunlight was the first time Lindsey was able to get a good look at Hermes—until then it had always been by candlelight. Though his face was deeply etched with lines by the sands of time, it was obvious he'd been a ruggedly handsome man in his youth.

"Take a seat here on the bank and wait while I secure a boat to take us across," Hermes said. Lindsey sat on the hard ground not all that far from where she and Tiye had collected clay for the vessels a day earlier. She was tempted to venture off and explore, but she knew Hermes would be angry if she ignored his instructions.

Hermes finally returned, accompanied by an older man, with a weathered face and a twinkle in his eye. The man led them to a small boat tied to a wooden post driven into the riverbank and held out a calloused hand to help Lindsey into the vessel.

With Lindsey safely aboard, Hermes took his position opposite her as the boatsman dipped his oars into the water and began to row. Minutes later they were on the other side of the river. When she looked back, she thought about her conversation with Tiye the previous day. Tiye was right: Everything could be looked at in polar opposite ways.

"The river is beautiful is it not?" Hermes said. "The river has nourished our land for millennia." And it will for thousands more, Lindsey thought.

"How far do we have to walk to get there?" Lindsey asked.

"It is too far to walk. We shall use camels."

"Oh, no," she said sternly. "I'm not getting on a camel."

A minute later, Lindsey found herself hoisted onto a cushioned wooden saddle on the back of an eight-foot-tall camel. The good news was she and Hermes weren't riding alone. They were accompanied by a pair of experienced camel drivers responsible for ensuring a safe journey.

It didn't take long for Lindsey to discover that riding a camel was a lot different from riding a horse. Camels have a unique way of walking that creates a constant swaying motion. The rolling sensation was so disorienting they had to stop so she could vomit.

"First time on a camel?" Lindsey heard the camel driver ask through the LanguaSync device in her ear.

"She will become accustomed to the rhythm soon enough," Hermes said.

Once Lindsey's stomach was empty, she was helped back onto the camel and motioned to the camel driver that she was ready.

"You might have warned me about this," Lindsey said once they were underway. Hermes shot Lindsey a look, and she knew he was right. She was the one who asked to come.

* * *

A fter several hours of riding, the camel driver stopped and helped Hermes and Lindsey to the ground so they could rest and eat.

"How did you know I'd get used to the swaying motion of the camel?" Lindsey asked.

"All must become accustomed to the rhythms of the world if they wish to enjoy life," Hermes said.

"The rhythms of the world?"

"Yes. Everything flows, out and in; everything has its tides; all things rise and fall. Everything in the universe follows a natural rhythm—cyclical patterns of flow that repeat again and again. Day turns into night, and night turns into day. The rise and fall of ocean tides. The waxing and waning cycles of the moon. We understand this through the fifth law of the universe—The Law of Rhythm."

"There's an explanation for everything you just mentioned," Lindsey said.

"I did not say there wasn't," Hermes said.

* * *

L ike everything else one sees, hears, and experiences—there is a logical reason behind it," Hermes said. "What appears to be chaos at first glance is not chaotic at all; it is all by design. Nothing is by accident. Think about the changing of the seasons, the blossoming flowers of the spring, when we plant our crops, the growth of those crops into the abundance of summer that becomes the harvest of autumn, giving way finally to the hibernation of winter—and the cycle begins again. There are many patterns in the world, Lindsey. Do you see them?"

Lindsey thought about the rhythms of music, the beating of drums. Menstrual cycles. Moon phases. Traffic patterns. The boom-and-bust cycles of the stock market. The migration patterns of animals. And what about fads and fashions? How what was once popular gives way to the new, then those same styles resurface as nostalgia and become the new retro trend. The examples were endless.

"We inhale, we exhale. Our heart beats. We sleep, we wake, then sleep again," Hermes said. "Like the seasons of nature, there are seasons of life. We are born into the world as energetic infants. Grow into adulthood. Work and reproduce. Become old and die, only to be reborn in a different form of energy. This sequence of birth, death, and rebirth is true for all things, all people, and all societies."

"Is this why you don't want people to know the Pharaoh is dying?"

"Yes. Egypt is on the verge of a cataclysmic change."

* * *

"Tiye told me the first three laws of the universe were immutable, meaning they couldn't be changed," Lindsey said. "But the last four laws could be transcended. I'm not sure how the seasons can be changed—and there is no way to transcend death."

"Yes, the seasons come and go, and there is nothing we can do to change that. There is not a thing we can do to avoid death, either. Remembering that winter gives way to spring allows us to mentally transcend the impact of trying times. This ability to navigate rough waters is embodied in the mantra: This too shall pass."

"You're saying that all of life's circumstances are temporary, and knowing this helps us deal with them," Lindsey stated.

"Precisely. The good moments and the bad moments in life are fleeting. Understanding The Law of Rhythm encourages patience, builds resilience, and provides perspective. Imagine someone is going through a desperate time in their life: A health issue, grieving the loss of a loved one, or financial difficulties. Realizing that *this too shall pass* is a way of offering comfort and hope, reminding them that their current troubles will eventually improve or be overcome."

We don't transcend the events themselves, Lindsey thought. We learn to manage our thoughts and emotions to enhance our ability to deal with them.

Lindsey recalled how her grandmother would sing to her as a small child in the car on long drives to and from her parent's house: *Row, row, row your boat, gently down the stream. Merrily, merrily, merrily, merrily, life is but a dream.*

"And know this, Lindsey," Hermes continued. "The secret of The Law of Rhythm is to go with the tides as opposed to trying to resist them."

Lindsey thought about a time when she was under an enormous amount of stress in college. Demanding courses, writing reports, and taking exams, all while holding down two jobs. She felt like she was coming apart at the seams. But she made it through. Years later, when she came up with the idea for LanguaSync, her company was on the verge of bankruptcy. Exhaustion took over. She almost quit. But she didn't. Why? Because she had survived the stress before, in college. It was as if someone whispered in her ear: *This too shall pass, Lindsey. This too shall pass.*

"There is something else, Lindsey, something most people miss," Hermes said. "The Law of Rhythm teaches us to embrace both ends of the spectrum, both happy times *and* sad times. Our highs *and* our lows—our successes *and* our failures—each serve a purpose in our growth. Resisting the natural flows of life can cause unnecessary struggle and suffering. We must learn to surrender to the currents of the river. When we stop resisting, we find that the river will take us effortlessly forward."

* * *

After a few more hours of riding, Hermes and Lindsey arrived at the Pharaoh's tomb, which was little more than a concealed doorway, hidden beneath the desert surface to deter tomb robbers. Had it not been for workers scrabbling about like worker ants and dozens of the Pharaoh's Royal Guards, no one would know the place was even there.

The guards were dressed in purple and red tunics and wore leather sandals like the guards who chased Lindsey through the marketplace. Each carried what appeared to be swords made of bronze, wooden shields, and head coverings adorned with the image of a cobra.

"What does the cobra mean?" Lindsey asked as they were helped to the ground by the camel driver.

"The cobra symbolizes protection," Hermes said. "Wait here."

Lindsey watched as Hermes approached the guards and produced a piece of parchment paper from his pocket, which Lindsey assumed was some kind of permission to enter the tomb. The guards studied the paper, then Hermes turned around and came back to where Lindsey waited.

"I must go in by myself," Hermes said, removing the LanguaSync device from his ear and placing it in Lindsey's hand. "Stay covered and wait here by the camels. The guards will leave you alone as they know you are with me."

"Why can't I go in?"

"The guards forbid a woman to enter the Pharaoh's tomb," Hermes said.

* * *

A wave of disappointment washed over Lindsey. She'd traveled all day—by camel, no less—only to be turned away and forced to stand in the burning sun because she was a woman.

Then she had an idea.

Lindsey leaned in close to Hermes and quietly said, "Tiye wanted me to tell you to be courageous, whatever that means." Hermes nodded in understanding.

Lindsey's heart was pounding as she watched Hermes disappear down the hidden stairway toward the tomb. She'd just done something dangerous, having dropped Hermes' LanguaSync device into the pocket of his robe. She might not be allowed to enter the tomb, but that didn't mean she couldn't listen.

* * *

The LanguaSync devices were designed with the ability to transmit and receive at reasonable distances, but they were never intended to work through the stone walls of a tomb in the middle of the desert. A moment later, Lindsey was thrilled to hear the voices of the two men in her ear:

Hermes: "Pharaoh, I come to you per your request."

THE EIGHTH VESSEL

Thutmose III: "Come closer. Have you completed the task you were assigned?"

Hermes: "The scrolls are almost completed. Each scroll will be placed in one of seven vessels and brought here for your journey to the afterlife. However, I come to you with a request."

Thutmose III: "I am in no condition to—"

Hermes: "My request requires no action. I wish to inform you I have made a second set of the laws, and I seek your blessing in distributing this knowledge to the common people."

Thutmose III: "You dare to suggest such a thing? The scrolls are meant for me and my bloodline alone. How could you think of betraying the sacred trust I have bestowed upon you?"

Hermes: "Pharaoh, I do not seek to betray you, but sharing your wisdom with all your subjects would elevate our civilization."

Thutmose III: "You speak of the greater good, Hermes, but in doing so, you have betrayed the very essence of your role. You have overstepped, and I can no longer trust you. I forbid you from taking this action."

Lindsey held her breath, wondering what Hermes would do. Would he stand up to the Pharoah? Or would he relent?

Hermes: "As you wish, Pharaoh. I have made my request and will honor your command."

Chapter XIII:
The Sixth Vessel

The Law of Cause and Effect
"Every Cause Has Its Effect; Every Effect Has Its Cause."

THE EIGHTH VESSEL

The tension in the scriptorium was palpable. Hermes was angry with Lindsey, and with good reason: She'd listened in on the man's private conversation with the Pharaoh the previous day in the Valley of the Kings. Hermes had not said a word to her since.

Tiye, on the other hand, was livid at Hermes for telling the Pharaoh about their plan to distribute the Seven Laws of the Universe to the people.

Ancient Egyptian society was hierarchical, with the Pharaoh at the top, followed by priests, nobility, and government officials. Knowledge, including the ability to read and write, was reserved by law for these elite members of society. Everyone else—farmers, laborers, and craftsmen—were held down. The commoners were also heavily taxed and forced to work vast tracts of land owned by the elites, which filled their stomachs with food and their pockets with wealth. Tiye knew the only way to break the Pharaoh's iron grip over the people was through knowledge and had convinced Hermes to make a second copy of the scrolls. Now, the plan was in jeopardy.

"I do not understand you, Hermes," Tiye said. "We agreed to make copies of the laws that would be distributed after the Pharaoh's death. Then you go and tell him? You are the smartest man in all of Egypt, but also its biggest fool!"

"I did not have it in me to betray him," Hermes said. "You blame the Pharaoh for his faults without acknowledging all the good he has done."

"Good?"

"Yes, the good. Have you forgotten his many military conquests? His expansion of trade routes and resources? We live in a time of unparalleled wealth and prosperity because of Thutmose. Look at the art! Our land is dotted with obelisks, statues, and temples built with the greatest craftsmanship ever known to honor the grandeur of the Gods because of him."

"To honor the Gods? Hermes, please, he builds temples to honor himself and to remind people of his unbending power," Tiye said. "The lives of the Egyptian people are filled with death, disease, and unspeakable hardships. The laws of the universe belong to the people, and you would deny them that?"

"The laws are the possession of the Pharaoh," Hermes said flatly.

Tiye turned to Lindsey and said, "Do you see what I mean? Hermes is a wise sage, but not wise enough to find the courage to do the correct thing."

"We tried, and we failed," Hermes said.

"You failed, Hermes—you!" Tiye shouted. "I refuse to bend my knee to that tyrant. Do you not remember the life I lived before being granted my freedom? Well, I haven't! And I will use my last grains of freedom to help free others, while you use your weakness to keep them enslaved."

"Asking his permission was the correct course of action," Hermes said. "I stand by my decision."

"Yes, you stand by your decision," Tiye said. "Yet, sadly, you didn't have the courage to stand up to him."

* * *

Lindsey had sensed that Hermes and Tiye were up to something since the first day she'd arrived—toiling away in the middle of the night, the way they went quiet whenever she walked into the room—now she understood why. "You could still distribute the laws," Lindsey said cautiously.

"You know what will happen next," Tiye said, ignoring Lindsey and taking a step toward Hermes. "Your betrayal will burn in the pit of the Pharaoh's stomach, and he will send his guards for you—you will be locked away, or worse."

The words *or worse* hung in the air, and Lindsey shivered at the thought of what fate Hermes might be facing.

Tiye's words turned out to be prophetic, as minutes later the Pharaoh's guards stormed into the temple, and Hermes was placed in chains.

"Where are the vessels?" one of the guards demanded.

"The vessels are not here," Tiye lied. "Even if they were, they have yet to be sealed. Would you dare bring the vessels to the Pharaoh in an unsealed state?"

The guards shared a nervous look, then asked: "When will they be ready?"

"Tomorrow," Tiye said.

"We will come for them at daylight. Have the vessels ready, or we shall put the two of you in chains as well."

Once the guards had taken Hermes away, Lindsey said: "You lied to the guards, didn't you?"

"Only half of what I said was a lie," Tiye said. "The vessels are here, but they have yet to be sealed. We shall finish the task this evening."

* * *

Sealing the vessels was far more involved than Lindsey had expected. "The vessels must be airtight to prevent the papyrus from degrading due to air and moisture," Tiye said. "It is a process Hermes invented. We call it Hermetic Sealing."

Lindsey had heard the term a thousand times and had never considered its origin.

"I have already inserted the scrolls in the vessels," Tiye said. "We now must prepare the epoxy."

The epoxy itself was a clear liquid that hardened when mixed with a second liquid that initiated the curing process. Tiye placed the two liquids in a bowl and mixed them together with a stick, instantly causing fumes to fill the air. It seemed to Lindsey it would have been wise to wear gloves and safety glasses to protect their skin and eyes, but like many things, they had yet to be invented.

Tiye handed the stick to Lindsey. "Stir the liquid until the bubbles have disappeared, then we must allow the liquid to cure."

"You were right about the Pharaoh having Hermes arrested," Lindsey said. "How did you know?"

"The Pharaoh is a vindictive man," Tiye said. "He would never let such a betrayal go unpunished. It was a simple matter of cause and effect, which happens to be the sixth law of the universe."

Lindsey couldn't argue with the statement. Hermes' actions of telling the truth caused the Pharaoh's actions, plain and simple. It was a logical chain of events. If you heat water, it will eventually boil at a predictable 212 degrees. Bury an acorn, it will grow into an oak tree. Don't sleep for three days and watch the impact on your ability to function. Don't study or pass the tests and you'll probably fail the course. Eat too much sugar, don't brush your teeth, don't invest money for retirement, run stop signs, and just see what happens.

There were many times in Lindsey's life when things were in complete chaos, and she wondered why such things were happening *to* her. When she looked with an honest, objective eye, she had caused it all through her own thoughts, emotions, and actions.

* * *

"Manifesting one's future through The Law of Cause and Effect requires more than mere thinking," Tiye said as she checked the epoxy again. "Since the day I first suggested it to him, Hermes thought about releasing the laws of the universe to the people, but it remained just that—*a thought*. Thinking *is* a cause, but thinking alone does not create change. There is also doing."

Lindsey could see why Tiye was so frustrated with Hermes.

"Mental imaginings are instantly created on the spiritual plane," Tiye continued, "but for things to manifest in the physical plane, there is much more to it. You must form a clear mental picture and then hold the image continuously in your mind. And behind your clear vision, there must be a purpose. If there is not a burning desire for the thing that you want to attract, you will not have the perseverance to pursue it. And you must have unwavering, invincible faith and belief that the thing you want is already yours. The truth is, everything is already here in one form or another. If we become a vibrational match to that which we desire most, then we cannot help but bring it into our material existence."

"Like the way you broke free from being a slave," Lindsey said.

Tiye nodded. "Yes, but there is something else that must be present. To manifest what you want, you must be grateful for everything you have ever received in the past, everything you have in the present, and for everything that has yet to come your way in the future. Gratitude is the connecting link between the finite man and the Infinite Source of all."

"Gratitude—even *before* its arrival?" Lindsey asked.

"Yes, if you believe in karma," Tiye said. "Karma is the universe's way of restoring balance. One needs to take the wanted with the unwanted, remembering even the unwanted can be seen as good if you choose. You do something nice for someone, and they don't return the kindness, but then a stranger does something unexpectedly kind to you. Karma is neither good nor bad, Lindsey. Karma simply is the reaction to the action. For every action there is an equal reaction in the opposite direction. Send out love, and the universe will return it—but not always in the form you expect, and not always in the timeframe you desire. There can be a lag in time for those thoughts and actions to become reality. Time is a man-made social construct, anyway."

Lindsey thought about how people would watch *The Secret* and believe all they had to do was wish for things and those things would magically arrive. Not that that couldn't happen, sometimes it did—but in most instances, more effort was required. After all, it was right there in plain sight: The Law of Attr**action**.

* * *

Once the epoxy had cured to the desired hardness, Tiye showed Lindsey how to apply the resin to the edges of round pieces of copper that had been cut to fit the necks of the vessels. Then Tiye pulled seven gemstones from the pocket of her robe and set them on the table. Their beauty made Lindsey catch her breath.

"What are these?" Lindsey gasped.

"Gemstones have spiritual and symbolic significance in our culture," Tiye said. "One of these stones is to be attached to the seal of each vessel."

Tiye pointed to a shiny black stone. "This is obsidian, used to guard the dead. The blue stone is lapis lazuli, a symbol of the sky and divine power. The turquoise stone symbolizes joy and rebirth. Carnelian is associated with life force and vitality. Jasper represents protection and strength. The green stone is malachite, a stone of transformation, which symbolizes positive change, spiritual enlightenment, and wisdom. This is serpentine, to ward off venomous bites from snakes and scorpions and to provide protection and healing."

"And the final stone?" Lindsey asked.

"This is amethyst," Tiye said. "It heightens consciousness and symbolizes freedom from ignorance."

Tiye took one of the circular pieces of copper and pushed it into the neck of the first vessel. Satisfied the vessel was properly sealed, Tiye dabbed epoxy on the obsidian gemstone and affixed it to the top of the vessel. Then she did the same for the next six vessels.

It was only then that Lindsey noticed there was an eighth vessel. "There are eight vessels, not seven. Why?"

"The extra vessel was made in case one of the others should break," Tiye said. "Do not concern yourself with it."

Chapter XIV:
The Seventh Vessel

The Law of Gender
"Gender Is in Everything; Everything Has Its Masculine and Feminine Principles; Gender Manifests on All Planes."

THE EIGHTH VESSEL

The sound of knocking on the door pulled Lindsey from a deep sleep. When she opened it, Tiye was standing there. "Ana bihajat alaa musaeadatikum," she heard Tiye say as the woman slipped into the room and quickly closed the door behind her.

At first, Lindsey thought she didn't understand Tiye because she didn't have a LanguaSync in her ear, but then realized she did. The battery was dead. Fortunately, she had two extra devices with her.

"I need your help," Lindsey heard Tiye say once she exchanged the dead device for a live one.

"Of course," Lindsey said. "What do you need?"

"I went to see Hermes, but the guards turned me away because I had nothing to bribe them with. Will you give me your gold chain?"

Lindsey retrieved the Cartier necklace from the table and held it out to Tiye. "Do you think it will be enough for them to let you in?"

Tiye nodded. "I have nothing to offer you in return."

"It's okay, you gave me your amulet, remember?" Lindsey said.

Tiye reached out and placed her hand on Lindsey's shoulder. "Be careful," she said. "The moments ahead will be fraught with peril. It would be best if you returned to your home."

*　*　*

Lindsey knew Tiye was right—it was time for her to leave. She'd considered using the copper mirror in the scriptorium to get back, but either Hermes or Tiye was always there. But they wouldn't be there now. Hermes was locked deep below the temple, and Tiye was on her way to see him. This might be her only chance.

Lindsey considered changing into her original clothing but thought better of it. If the guards happened to see her, they would most certainly arrest her. She covered her head with her scarf and placed her phone, gold Bulgari bracelet, and Tiffany diamond earrings in the pocket of her robe. Everything else was left behind.

Lindsey passed near the courtyard. The air was cool and still and filled with the sound of birds chirping in the distance as the pink and purple colors of sunrise appeared on the horizon. It wouldn't be long before the guards would come to collect the vessels. She needed to hurry.

Unfortunately, the Pharaoh's guards were everywhere, standing at the entrance of every room like unyielding sentinels, their eyes alert and watchful. Getting into the scriptorium was out.

Lindsey walked further down the hall, toward the room with the vessels, and watched as the guards carefully carried them down the hallway toward her. The light from the torches glinted off the gemstones on the vessels as they walked past: obsidian, lapis lazuli, turquoise, carnelian, jasper, malachite, and, lastly, serpentine. The eighth vessel was not among them.

Once the guards were gone, Lindsey walked to the doorway and glanced into the room. It was empty. The eighth vessel was gone, as well. There was only one thing she could assume.

Tiye had taken it.

* * *

Lindsey knew it was probably a stupid thing to do, but she desperately wanted to talk with Hermes. The last time they were together, it did not end well with the guards placing him in chains and dragging him away. For all she knew, he was gone, but she thought it was worth a try.

Tiye had taught her how to get past the guards.

Bribe them.

When Lindsey reached the room where Hermes was being held, she was relieved to see two of the Pharaoh's guards standing at attention by the door, suggesting Hermes was still there. There was no reason to guard an empty room.

Lindsey was wearing her LanguaSync under her scarf, so she could understand the guards, but they wouldn't be able to understand her. She decided the best course of action was to say nothing and hope they understood.

As she approached the door, the guard closest to her stepped forward, drew his sword, and said, "Stop where you are."

Lindsey wasted no time and pulled the diamond earrings from her pocket and held them up for the guard to see. Then she pointed at the door to the room and waited. The guards glanced at each other, then each of them took one of the studs. Seconds later, Lindsey was in the room with Hermes.

The first thing Lindsey did was to hand Hermes the only remaining LanguaSync, hoping the battery was still working. It was.

"You have taken a great risk coming here," Hermes said.

"I wanted to tell you something," Lindsey said. "It's important.

"Yes?"

"Tiye had an eighth vessel made."

"Did this eighth vessel have a gemstone?" Hermes asked. "Was the stone an amethyst?"

"How did you know?" Lindsey asked.

"Amethyst symbolizes freedom from ignorance. It would be the gemstone Tiye would use to let me know she'd taken the second copy of the laws. I'm sure she intends to release them."

"You don't seem angry," Lindsey said. "You're acting like you expected it."

"Did Tiye tell you about her upbringing?" Hermes asked.

Lindsey nodded.

"Tiye possesses a strength I have never had. When I took her under my wing, I asked her if she could have anything in the world, what would it be? She told me she wanted to be a scribe."

"Like you."

"Yes," Hermes said. "Unfortunately, when the time came, her request was denied by the Council of Elites. Gender should not determine what one is allowed to do with their life, but we do not have an equal balance of masculine and feminine energies in our institutions. Sadly, not everyone in Egypt is allowed to express those qualities. I lobbied the Pharaoh to make an exception for Tiye, but he turned a deaf ear to my request. From that moment on, Tiye hated the Pharaoh, and I feared that she hated me, as well."

"She didn't," Lindsey said.

THE EIGHTH VESSEL

"Yes, I know that now," Hermes said. "Tiye came to see me this morning. Our leaders are blind to the truth—that everything and everyone in the universe has both masculine and feminine qualities. They believe it is one way or the other; that displaying any side of themselves other than their physical sex makes them look weak. They are wrong. True power arises from honoring and embracing the opposite sides within oneself. Each of us has aspects of both genders within us, and each person should be able to express their authentic selves because the balance between these two energies is essential for harmony and creation."

Lindsey had always believed that—while she was technically a female—she possessed some masculine energies, especially when it came to building her business. And while her husband, Jack, was physically a male, he also displayed some female energies. Neither of them was 100 percent feminine nor masculine, but they complemented each other well.

Many times, Lindsey had thought about how the agenda of the elites in modern times was to confuse the masses with this law. Instead of honoring the sacred balance between the two, the world has fictitiously invented dozens of pretend genders to create division among people. There is a full-on war on The Law of Gender now, more than ever before. Instead of people honoring themselves as they are created and embracing contrasting energies, they have come to believe they must physically alter themselves to match the mental disorientation within. An excess in either direction creates disorder and disharmony and ultimately creates a contradiction in nature.

* * *

"Did Tiye tell you she was going to take the scrolls?" Lindsey asked.

Hermes shook his head. "No, but she didn't have to. I have long known that when the moment came, Tiye would do the right thing rather than the easy thing. The right thing was always to share the knowledge of the universe with the people, and in that, I failed. Now, I fear *The Kybalion* will never see the light of day."

"What?" Lindsey exclaimed. "Did you say *The Kybalion?*"

"Yes," Hermes said. "*The Kybalion* was the name we gave to the manuscript we were working on; an exact copy of everything contained in the scrolls. It was to be distributed to the people, and it would have been had I not been such a coward."

Lindsey could not believe what she was hearing. "You are Hermes Trismegistus, aren't you?"

"Yes, that is my full name. Did Tiye tell you that?"

"No," Lindsey said, so excited she could barely catch her breath. She hadn't put it together until that moment. Hermes Trismegistus was a legendary figure in the world of philosophy and spiritual wisdom. *He* was the author of the laws of the universe—also known as the Hermetic teachings. "I know because I've read *The Kybalion*. As you and Tiye were sharing your knowledge the last few days, I recognized so much of what you were saying, but—"

"You have read *The Kybalion?*" Hermes asked, puzzled. "How is that possible?"

Lindsey realized there could only be one answer:

Tiye.

Tiye escaped with the manuscript, but *The Kybalion* wasn't published until 1908. Why did it take so long? Where had it been for all that time? Again, there was only one answer. Tiye escaped and hid the eighth vessel with the manuscript inside, but for some reason, she was unable to retrieve it. Had she been caught and jailed? Lindsey shuddered at the thought. But it was the only logical way things could have happened.

"Tell me, how is it possible—?" Hermes asked again, but Lindsey remained silent. Finally, Hermes understood.

"It was Tiye," Hermes said.

Lindsey nodded and said, "*The Kybalion* is one of the most important books in history, the content in it is referred to as the Seven Hermetic Principles, providing the framework for understanding and applying the seven universal laws. You didn't fail Hermes, you succeeded beyond your wildest dreams!"

"The book has my name on it?" Hermes asked. "We wrote anonymously saying it was by The Two Initiates. Tiye must have changed it."

"Why would Tiye change it from The Two Initiates to The Three—?"

Lindsey stopped midsentence when she understood: Tiye had given Lindsey credit for being the third initiate. It was an honor beyond anything she could ever have imagined, and she burst into tears.

"The guards will be coming back soon," Hermes said. "You must go."

Lindsey wiped her face with the sleeve of her robe and said, "What about you? What is going to happen?"

Hermes reached into the pocket of his robe and produced a dagger—the same one Tiye had threatened Lindsey with when she first arrived. "Take this, you may need it," Hermes said. "Tiye slipped it to me when she visited earlier, but I have no need for it. There is no escaping my destiny. My fate is sealed."

CHAPTER XV:
Back to the Present

When the guards came to take Lindsey from the room where Hermes was being held, they looked at her in a strange way. Something was wrong. The guards spoke to each other, but the only word she understood was the word, *yellow*.

Lindsey glanced down and instantly understood what had caused the guard's reaction: A lock of her blonde hair had fallen from beneath her scarf and was visible on her shoulder. She made it halfway up the tunnel, hoping maybe they would simply let her go. No such luck.

She started running.

Fortunately, Lindsey had an advantage. She'd spent much of the last week finding her way through the labyrinth of tunnels that wound beneath the temple. Moments later, she'd lost them.

Lindsey found her way to the scriptorium and was relieved to see the copper mirror where she'd seen it last, leaning against the far wall of the room. The question now was, would this mirror work the same way the obsidian mirror had at home?

Lindsey stood before the mirror, torchlight dancing off the walls, and took a deep breath, then began repeating the incantation she'd used to get there ten days earlier:

> "Through this mirror, I seek to find,
> the realm beyond all space and time.
> As above is so below,
> take me where I'd like to go."

But nothing happened.

Lindsey repeated the incantation a second time, and then a third, all without success. Then, she heard the guards coming down the tunnel toward the scriptorium. She looked over and saw that in her haste, she'd failed to close the door.

It was too late now.

Lindsey returned her gaze toward the mirror and with all the conviction she could muster, she said:

> "Reveal the path forward to the year
> 2024. I ask to be returned to my home.
> Please return me home!"

Two guards appeared in the doorway and watched in confusion as the copper mirror began to radiate the ethereal glow it had in the meditation room at home. The looks of confusion turned to looks of fear as the mirror began to rattle and shake against the wall. Afraid the mirror was going to topple over, Lindsey reached out and placed her hands on the surface to steady it...

And then she fell through.

* * *

Lindsey found herself floating weightlessly through a dark void, then was suddenly thrown into the meditation room with such force Jack heard the noise from the room below. A minute later, he entered and found her sprawled on the floor wearing a dirty robe and leather sandals and smelling terrible.

As expected, Jack was confused and desperate to know where she'd been. So was the FBI, which had spent four days at the house waiting for a ransom call that never came. After pressing her repeatedly for an explanation without getting any answers, they gave up and left. All Lindsey would say was, "I don't know" and "I don't remember anything." Telling them she'd traveled through a mirror to Ancient Egypt was out of the question; she had no desire to be institutionalized.

When she finally felt ready to tell Jack what had happened, he took it better than expected. "So, you believe me?" she asked. Jack replied: "Do I have any choice?" The fact that Lindsey had been dressed in a robe and wearing leather sandals helped.

Lindsey stood there for a long time, silently looking at herself in the mirror. Then she said: "I want to go to Egypt."

"I don't understand," Jack said. "If what you're telling me is true, you just got back from there."

"That's the point," Lindsey said. "I want to prove that what happened was real."

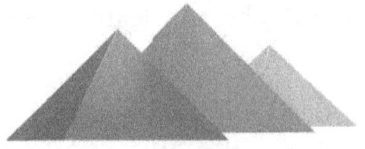

CHAPTER XVI
Returning to Egypt

Before the trip, Lindsey buried herself in research on Ancient Egypt. Some research was done online but was too general. The details she was seeking to validate her experience just weren't there. Eventually, she decided to look elsewhere.

She read every book written by reputable Egyptologists, watched every documentary on Netflix and Amazon Prime, and visited The University of Chicago and the Bancroft Library at UC Berkley. Each had extensive collections of books, journals, and academic papers on Ancient Egypt. At no time did Lindsey share her experiences with the experts she met with, though she was tempted to correct them on some of their information that she knew was wrong. But the goal of her research was to *discover* information, not share it.

One of the experts she talked to recommended she contact Dr. Kent Weeks, famous for his work in the Valley of the Kings. He'd made international headlines by discovering the tomb of Ramesses II's sons, some seventy feet below the surface of Egypt's Valley of the Kings. Unfortunately, Dr. Weeks was 81 years of age and wasn't taking meetings.

Eventually, she was ready for her and Jack to make the trip to Egypt. This time she would be traveling by plane.

* * *

After a quick stop in London to peruse the Egyptology exhibition at the British Museum, they caught a direct flight to Cairo.

The museum in Cairo housed a vast collection of artifacts, including those from the reign of Pharaoh Thutmose III.

Thutmose III's tomb, known as KV34, was discovered in the Valley of the Kings by a team of French archaeologists in 1898. The mummy of the Pharaoh was discovered in a sarcophagus made of wood and red quartzite. It had been stripped of its gold and gemstones by robbers. There were also the remains of seven clay vessels that had been smashed by the robbers in search of anything of value.

There were many other artifacts of interest, including chairs, stools, and beds, to provide for needs in the afterlife. The body of Thutmose III itself was not on display.

What interested Lindsey most was the sarcophagus discovered next to Thutmose, believed to hold the body of the Pharaoh's scribe, Hermes Trismegistus. It was believed that Trismegistus had been buried in the tomb to look after the Pharaoh. Lindsey knew better. Hermes had been buried by Thutmose III's side so the Pharaoh could keep his eye on him.

Lindsey stared at Hermes' sarcophagus without moving, wiping tears from her face the entire time.

* * *

When Lindsey and Jack left the museum, they were supposed to catch a flight back home. But Lindsey asked if they could take an extra day and visit Luxor.

THE EIGHTH VESSEL

As the limo made its way from the airport into the city of Luxor, Lindsey's jaw hung open. "What is it?" Jack asked.

"I was here when it was Thebes," Lindsey murmured, remembering how the city had been filled with cobblestone roads, temples, and buildings with beautiful architecture. "Look at it, Jack. It's all hotels, billboards, gift shops, and Burger Kings. It's criminal."

"Times change," Jack said. "We're riding in an air-conditioned limousine on our way to the Marriott, sweetie—we could be riding a camel and sleeping in the desert."

Point taken.

After they checked in and took a nap, Lindsey wanted to explore. The concierge suggested they check out Luxor Temple Street in an area called Sharia Al-Karnak. It had changed the least over the years and provided the best glimpse into Luxor's history.

As they walked, it was hard to say things looked familiar, even with the narrow alleyways and streetside farmer's markets, so Lindsey suggested they head to the river.

Again, Lindsey was struck by the changes. No fishermen in rowboats. No women doing their laundry on the bank of the river. Just restaurants, gift shops, modern bridges, cargo ships, and cruise liners. The closest thing to what the area used to be was a booth where you could take a camel ride along the water.

She'd been there and done that already.

Lindsey wasn't sure what she expected to find, but whatever it was, she didn't find it. She felt sad and empty. But when they arrived back at the hotel, everything changed.

There, on the side of the building, was a bronze plaque engraved with the following words:

> **Historic Site:**
>
> **This building is located at the site of the original Temple of Ra, which stood here from 1730 BC until it was torn down in 1961 due to wind erosion and water damage sustained over the years.**

Directly next to the plaque was an advertisement for guided tours of the tunnels that ran under the hotel and surrounding streets.

As badly as Lindsey wanted to take the tour, she couldn't bring herself to do it. Knowing the temple had been there was all the validation she needed. Besides, she'd already cried enough for one trip. It was time to head home.

CHAPTER XVII

The Speech

Lindsey looked at her reflection in the mirror and reviewed the outfit she'd chosen for the speech—a tailored charcoal gray jacket over a burgundy blouse, with black slacks that were stylish and conveyed confidence and professionalism, without overdoing it. For shoes, she wore a simple pair of flats. Lindsey knew she would rock the stage with her words—there was no need to dress over the top to gain the audience's approval. The experience she had in Ancient Egypt had changed her for the better. More than ever, she just wanted to authentically be herself, in the flow of life.

* * *

The phone dinged and Lindsey glanced down to see her Uber had arrived. Two hours later she was walking onstage at The Luxor for her talk.

It was hard for Lindsey to believe it had only been one month since she'd fallen through the mirror and found herself 3,500 years in the past. The question as to whether the experience was real had given way to acceptance. She'd asked herself why it had happened and had come to believe it was because she wanted it to happen. She stood before a mirror and asked to be transported to that place and time. Like Dorothy in the Wizard of Oz, wishing with all her might for the universe to grant her request, the universe responded.

After the applause died down, Lindsey said, "Before I begin, I'd like to ask everyone here a question, and that question is: What do you really want? I mean *really*—without talking yourself out of it or setting any limitations whatsoever. What is it you *really* want? I want you to think about this as we cover the Seven Laws of the Universe because as you begin to understand these, you will know exactly how to get what you want in life."

Lindsey slipped her hand into the pocket of her slacks and felt around until she found the ivory scarab Tiye had given her. Then she took a deep breath, and looked out at the audience and said, "Let's begin."

Notes of Interest

As stated in the introduction of this book, The Eighth Vessel is a work of historical fiction, yet much of the story is based on actual people, places, and events of historical significance.

THE CHARACTER "HERMES"

The character Hermes is based on Hermes Trismegistus, a legendary figure in ancient Greco-Egyptian mythology, believed to have been a wise mystic, philosopher, and alchemist. While there is no concrete evidence to establish exactly when Hermes Trismegistus may have lived, there is much to suggest he lived in Ancient Egypt around the time of the Pharaoh Thutmose III.

During this period, scribes like Hermes held esteemed positions in society as they were responsible for preserving knowledge primarily reserved for the elites. The Hermetic texts attributed to Hermes Trismegistus have played a significant role in shaping Western thought and traditions throughout history. His teachings on the nature of the divine have withstood the test of time.

HERMETIC SEALING

The process of sealing the vessels in this book is based on creating an airtight seal, typically used in containers or enclosures, associated with Hermes Trismegistus. The term 'hermetic' is also used to describe hidden wisdom known only to a select group of people and not widely understood by the public at large.

THE KYBALION

The Kybalion, first published in 1908, is the classic spiritual and philosophical text based on the principles of Hermetic Philosophy of Ancient Egypt and Greece. The book outlines seven principles considered to be the laws governing the universe.

THE THREE "INITIATES"

The true authors of *The Kybalion* are unknown, choosing to remain anonymous, referring to themselves simply as "The Three Initiates." The term *initiate* refers to someone formally admitted into a particular group or society, usually through a ceremonial process known as *initiation*. In a spiritual context, an initiate is someone who has achieved spiritual transformation by attaining a high level of knowledge not available to others.

PHARAOH THUTMOSE III

Thutmose III was one of the most famous Pharaohs of Ancient Egypt, often referred to as the "Napoleon of Egypt" due to his military prowess and the vast expansion of the Egyptian Empire during his reign from 1479 to 1425 BC. He was buried in the Valley of the Kings, on the west bank of the Nile near Luxor, Egypt, where many Pharaohs and nobles from that period were also interred. His tomb was discovered in 1898 by the archaeologist Victor Loret. The tomb contained the mummies and coffins of high-ranking individuals placed there to serve him in the afterlife. He was fifty-six at the time of his death.

ABOUT EGYPTIAN GEMSTONES

Ancient Egyptians used gemstones for various purposes, and these precious materials held significant cultural, religious, and practical value. Elites not only adorned themselves with jewelry made from gemstones while they were alive, but gemstones were often discovered hidden within the layers of mummy wrappings for protection in the afterlife.

ABOUT THE CHARACTER "TIYE"

While the character Tiye is purely fictional, life for women in Ancient Egypt during the reign of Thutmose III was highly influenced by one's social and economic status. Women from lower social classes were involved in various forms of labor, including agricultural work, pottery-making, weaving, and household tasks, while women from higher social classes might engage in managing estates and businesses. And, while women of high social status had access to education, it was not widely available to the poor, especially slaves. It was with this in mind that the character Tiye was created.

About the Author...

Jenna Zwagil grew up in a dusty little town in the inland deserts of California. She bounced around from one meaningless job to another and, from all outside appearances, had few prospects for a successful life. But Jenna had a burning desire to do and be more. Her senior yearbook 10-year prediction was: *Retired as a Business Owner.*

The only problem was she hadn't figured out what that business was supposed to be. Even as obstacles piled up around her as fast as her debt, she didn't give up. Then, during the summer of 2014, Jenna met Josh Zwagil, who was about to launch MyDailyChoice (aka, MDC) a network marketing company. Jenna joined as one of the first affiliates.

After three rollercoaster years in the MDC start-up, Jenna discovered CBD oil and was convinced that it was not only a product she needed but something that the market needed, as well. She called the company HempWorx, and it turns out she was right. The market for their product was ready to explode.

MDC merged with HempWorx in 2017, and in that same year, Jenna and Josh merged their relationship as husband and wife, as well. Today, they are at the helm of a business with over $100 million in sales in 2022 and continue to grow.

Beyond her work inside the company, Jenna has a passion for mentorship. She loves sharing the hard-fought lessons she's learned both on her personal journey and through reading and studying the works of the greatest personal development teachers of all time. Her first book, *Breaking All the Rules*, was an Amazon Bestseller.

Connect With Jenna:

Facebook FAN PAGE @jennazwagil

Instagram @jennazwagil

Thank you for reading!

I hope you loved it and would deeply appreciate it if you'd post a review on your favorite book buying platform.

Also by Jenna Zwagil

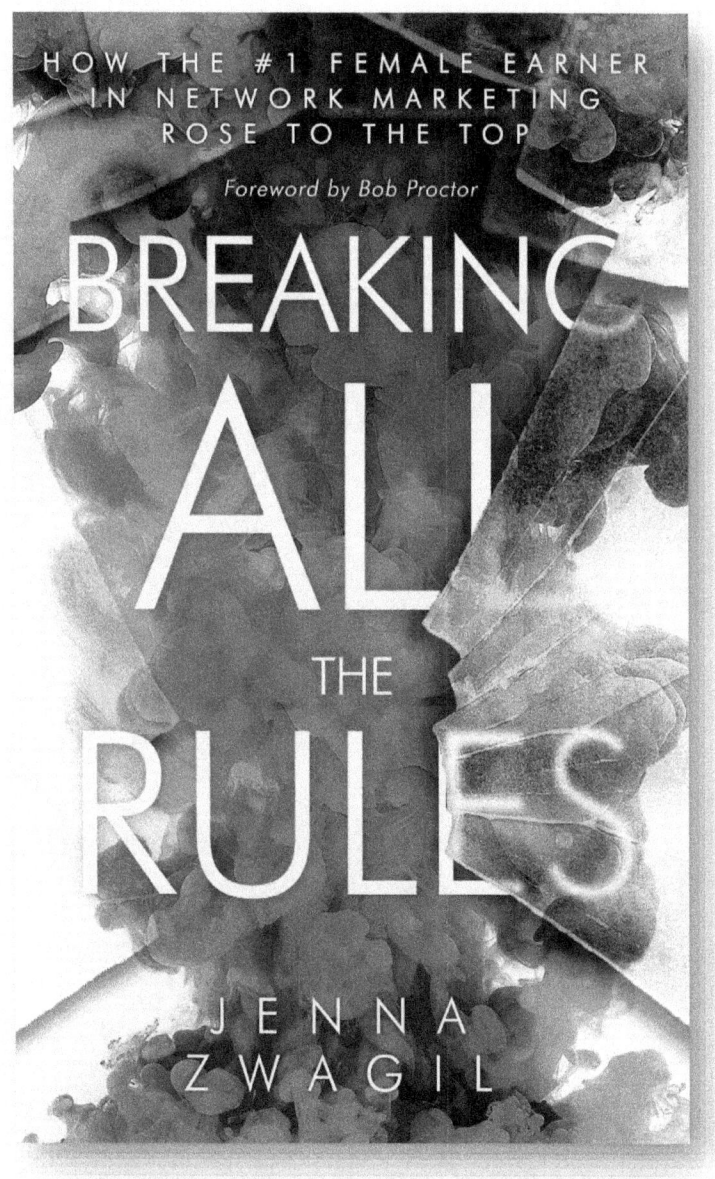

www.ingramcontent.com/pod-product-compliance
Lightning Source LLC
LaVergne TN
LVHW051844080426
835512LV00018B/3053